INSIGHT GUIDES

P9-AQU-846

SWEDISH

PHRASEBOOK & DICTIONARY

No part of this book may be reproduced, stored in a retrieval system or transmitted in any form or means electronic, mechanical, photocopying, recording or otherwise, without prior written permission from APA Publications.

Contacting the Editors

Every effort has been made to provide accurate information in this publication, but changes are inevitable. The publisher cannot be responsible for any resulting loss, inconvenience or injury. We would appreciate it if readers would call our attention to any errors or outdated information. We also welcome your suggestions; if you come across a relevant expression not in our phrase book, please contact us at: hello@insightguides.com

All Rights Reserved
© 2015 APA Publications (UK) Ltd.

First Edition: 2015
Printed in China

Cover & Interior Design: Pawel Pasternak
Production: AM Services
Production Manager: Vicky Glover
Picture Researcher: Slawek Krajewski
Cover Photo: all iStockphoto

Interior Photos: all iStockphoto

CONTENTS

FOOD & DRINK

GOING OUT

DICTIONARY

PRONUNCIATION

This section is designed to familiarize you with the sounds of Swedish using our simplified phonetic transcription. You'll find the pronunciation of the Swedish letters and sounds explained below, together with their 'imitated' equivalents. To use this system, found throughout the phrase book, simply read the pronunciation as if it were English, noting any special rules below.

The Swedish alphabet has 29 letters, the last three of which are the vowels å, ä and ö. Unlike English, the letter y is a vowel, meaning that Swedish has nine vowels. Swedish vowels are pure vowel sounds, as opposed to being a combination of two sounds (diphthongs) as they often are in English. Diphthongs occur only in dialects such as **Gotländska** (spoken on the island of Gotland), **Skånska** (spoken in the southern province of Skåne) and **Dalmål** (spoken in Dalarna, a province roughly in the middle of the country).

Swedish has very consistent rules with respect to the sounding of individual letters, i.e. all the letters should be pronounced distinctly, even vowels and consonants at the ends of words. The Swedish language is often referred to as a 'musical' language due to the fact that the intonation and rhythm moves up and down, giving the language a musical quality. Despite this stress, pronunciation is quite consistent. Most words with two or more syllables have primary stress on the first syllable of the word, and this can be followed by a secondary stress on the second syllable. There are also a number of words with two or more syllables which do not have stress on the first syllable, but often on the last. Stress has been noted in the phonetic transcription with underlining.

CONSONANTS

Letter	Approximate Pronunciation	Symbol	Example	Pronunciation
c	like s in sit	s	cykel	<u>sew</u> • kerl*
g	1. before o, å, a and u, like g in get	g	gata	<u>gah</u> • ta
	2. before i, e, ö and ä, like y in yet	y	get	<u>yet</u>
	3. after r and l, like y in yet	y	borg	bohry
j	1. soft, like y in yet	y	jag	yahg
	2. after r and l, like y in yet	y	familj	fah • <u>mihly</u>
k	1. before o, å, a and u, like k in keep	k	katt	kat
	2. before i, e, ö and ä, like ch in chew		köpa	<u>chur</u> • pa
q	like k in keep	k	Blomquist	<u>bloom</u> • kvihst
r	strong, almost trilled, r		röd	rurd
s	like s in see	s	sitta	<u>siht</u> • a
w	like v in very	v	wennergren	<u>vehn</u> • eh • <u>grehn</u>
z	like s in suit	s	zebra	<u>see</u> • bra

Letters b, d, f, h, m, n, p, t, v and x are pronounced as in English.
*Bold indicates a lengthening of the sound — emphasis on the vowel sound.

CONSONANT CLUSTERS

Letter	Approximate Pronunciation	Symbol	Example	Pronunciation
ch	like sh in ship	**sh**	**check**	*shehk*
ck	like ck in tick	**k**	**flicka**	*<u>flih</u> • ka*
dj, gj, hj, lj	like y in yet	**y**	**djur**	*yeur*
sj, skj, stj, sch, ch	like sh in shop	**sh**	**sjal**	*shahl*
sk	1. before o, å, a and u, like sk in skip	**sk**	**skala**	*<u>skah</u> • la*
	2. before i, e, ö and ä, like sh in ship	**sh**	**skära**	*<u>shai</u> • ra*
tj	like sh followed by ch	**shch**	**tjock**	*shchohk*

VOWELS

Letter	Approximate Pronunciation	Symbol	Example	Pronunciation
a	1. when long, like a in father	**ah**	**dag**	*dahg*
	2. when short, like a in cat	**a**	**katt**	*kat*
e	1. when long, like ee in beer	**ee**	**veta**	*<u>vee</u> • ta*
	2. when short, like e in fell	**eh**	**ett**	*eht*

Letter	Approximate Pronunciation	Symbol	Example	Pronunciation
i	1. when long, like ee in see	ee	bil	*beel*
	2. when short, like i in bit	ih	mitt	*miht*
o	1. when long, like oa in coat	oa	sko	*skoa*
	2. like the exclamation oh	oh	font	*fohnt*
u	1. when long, eu in feud	eu	ruta	*reu • ta*
	2. when short, like u in up	uh	uppe	*uh • per*
y	like ew in new	ew	byta	*bew • ta*
å	1. when long, like oa in oar	oa	gå	*goa*
	2. when short, like o in hot	oh	åtta	*oh • ta*
ä	1. when long, like ai in air	ai	här	*hair*
	2. when short, like e in set	eh	säng	*sehng*
ö	1. when long, like u in cure	ur	smör	*smur*
	2. when short, like u in nut	uh	rött	*ruhrt*

Swedish vowels are divided into two groups: hard and soft. **A, o, u** and **å** are hard vowels; **e, i, y, ä** and **ö** are soft vowels. Vowels can also be pronounced either long or short. When a vowel is pronounced 'long' the sound is longer, but also more open and rounder. The 'short' vowel sounds are more closed, literally a 'shorter' sound than a long vowel. An easy rule to remember is that if the vowel is followed by a single consonant, as in **stad** (city), it is long. If the vowel is followed by a double consonant, as in **katt** (cat), the vowel is short. The exception to this rule is with the consonants **m** and **n**.

Swedish is spoken throughout Sweden as well as in the coastal regions of Finland and Estonia. While written Swedish has been standardized, there are characteristic spoken dialects in certain regions such as Gotland, Skåne and Dalarna. Other languages, in addition to Swedish, are also spoken in Sweden, such as Finnish, which is spoken in some communities in Northern Sweden, and the Sámi (Lappish) languages, which are spoken in Sámi communities throughout Northern Norway, Sweden, Finland and Russia. Swedish, Norwegian, Danish, Icelandic and Faroese (spoken on the Faroe Islands) are all derived from Old Norse, the language spoken prior to the Viking Age. Over time, the Scandinavian languages developed from this common language. Danish, Norwegian and Swedish are separate and distinct languages but remain close enough that they are mutually intelligible. The Finnish and Sámi languages belong to a different language family, to which Hungarian also belongs.

HOW TO USE THE APP

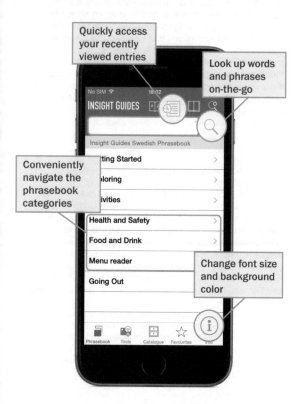

Quickly access your recently viewed entries

Look up words and phrases on-the-go

Conveniently navigate the phrasebook categories

Change font size and background color

Save the most useful everyday words and phrases to your Favorites

Use the Flash Cards Quiz to learn and memorize new words easily

Take all digital advantages of the app: listen to words and phrases pronounced by native speakers

Insight Guides Swedish Phrasebook

Is there a traditional Swedish/
inexpensive restaurant nearby?

Finns det något ... s /
någon billigarere ... ng
i närheten?

fihns dee noa•gohtvairds•heus /
noa•gohn bihl•ih•ga•rer
rehs•teu•rangee nair•hee•tehn

Can you reco...   A table for......

Phrasebook   Tools   Catalogue   Favourites   Info

To learn how to
activate the app,
see the inside
back cover of this
phrasebook.

THE BASICS

GRAMMAR

REGULAR VERBS

The present tense of regular verbs in Swedish is formed by adding either -**r** or -**er** to the stem. If the stem ends in **a**, add an -**r**, if it ends in a consonant add -**er**. The past tense is formed by adding either -**de** or -**te** to the basic form. If the basic form ends in a **p**, **t**, **k** or **s**, add -**te**, if not then add -**de**. The future is formed by adding the present tense of **ska** (will) + the verb in the infinitive. This applies to all persons (e.g., I, you, he, she, it, etc.). Following are the present, past and future forms of the verbs **att köpa** (to buy) and **att fråga** (to ask). The different conjugation endings are in bold.

	PRESENT	PAST	FUTURE
att köpa (to buy)	köpe**r**	köp**te**	*ska köpa*
att fråga (to ask)	fråga**r**	fråga**de**	*ska fråga*

PRONOUNS

I	jag	it (common/neuter)	den/det
you (sing., inf,)	du	we	vi
he	han	you (pl.)	ni
she	hon	they	de

In Swedish there are two terms for 'you': **du** (singular/informal) and **ni** (plural/informal). Both are used when talking to relatives, friends, colleagues, children, between young people and in work situations. The plural form, **ni**, is used in more formal situations to refer to one or more persons. Its use has however become less frequent, so nowadays you will hear most people address each other with **du**.

IRREGULAR VERBS

There are a number of irregular verbs in Swedish; these must be memorized. Like regular verbs, however, the irregular verb form remains the same, irrespective of person. The table below shows the present, past and future conjugations for a number of important, useful irregular verbs.

	PRESENT	PAST	FUTURE
att vara (to be)	**är**	**var**	*ska vara*
att ha (to have)	**har**	**hade**	*ska ha*
att komma (to come) *komma*	**kommer**	**kom**	*ska*
att göra (to do)	**gör**	**gjorde**	*ska göra*
att gå (to go/walk)	**går**	**gick**	*ska gå*

sing. = singular, inf. = informal, pl. = plural

WORD ORDER

There are a number of irregular verbs in Swedish; these must be memorized. Like regular verbs, however, the irregular verb form remains the same, irrespective of person. The table below shows the present, past and future conjugations for a number of important, useful irregular verbs.

Swedish is similar to English in terms of word order for simple sentences, i.e. it follows the subject-verb-object pattern.
Example:
Sara läser en bok. Sara is reading a book.
When the sentence doesn't begin with a subject, the word order changes; the verb and the subject are inverted.
Example:
Nu läser Sara en bok. Now Sara is reading a book.
However, **nu** could just as well be placed at the end of the sentence, e.g. **Sara läser en bok nu.**
Questions are formed by reversing the order of the subject and verb:
Du ser katten. You see the cat.
Ser du katten? Do you see the cat?

NEGATIONS

A statement can be negated by inserting the word **inte** after the verb:
Jag talar svenska. I speak Swedish.
Jag talar inte svenska. I do not speak Swedish.

NOUNS & ARTICLES

The indefinite article (a, an) is expressed with **en** for common nouns and with **ett** for neuter nouns. Generally, common nouns can be both feminine and masculine (e.g. people, animals, etc.); neuter nouns have no gender (e.g. house, roof, etc.). However, there are several exceptions to this rule.

In Swedish, there are five different endings used to form plural nouns; three correspond to common gender nouns and two to neuter gender nouns. The following rules apply to nouns in the indefinite singular.

1. **en** words that end in -**a** take an -**or** ending
2. **en** words that end in -**e** take an -**ar** ending
3. **en** words with stress on the last vowel take an -**er** ending
4. **ett** words that end in a vowel take an -**n** ending
5. **ett** words that end in a consonant take no additional ending

Common gender nouns that end in a consonant are not covered by the rules above. These words will take either an -**ar** ending or an -**er** ending. The nouns which fall into this category will simply need to be memorized.

SINGULAR INDEFINITE	PLURAL INDEFINITE
en flicka (a girl)	flick*or*
en timme (an hour)	timm*ar*
en telefon (a telephone)	telefon*er*
ett konto (an account)	kont*on*
ett hus (a house)	hus
en bil (a car)	bil*ar*

Definite articles: where in English we say 'the car', the Swedes say the equivalent of 'car-the', i.e. they tag the definite article onto the end of the noun. In the singular, common nouns take an -**en** ending, neuter nouns an -**et** ending. In the plural, common nouns add an -**na** and neuter nouns take an -**en** ending, neuter nouns an -**et** ending. In the plural, common nouns add an -**na** and neuter nouns take an -**en**.

	SINGULAR	PLURAL
common gender	**katten**	**katterna**
	the cat	the cats
neuter gender	**tårget**	**tågen**
	the train	the trains

DEMONSTRATIVE ADJECTIVES

	SINGULAR	NEUTER	PLURAL
this/these	**min**	**mitt**	**mina**
these/those	**den**	**det**	**de**
	denna bil	**deta hus**	
	(this car)	(this house)	

POSSESSIVE ADJECTIVES

	COMMON	NEUTER	PLURAL
my	**min**	**mitt**	**mina**
your (sing.)	**din**	**ditt**	**dina**
our	**vår**	**vårt**	**våra**
his	**hans**	**ditt**	**dina**
hers		**hennes**	
its		**dess/dess**	
their		**deras**	
your (pl.)	**er**	**ert**	**era**

ADVERBS & ADVERBIAL EXPRESSIONS

Adverbs are generally formed by adding **-t** to the corresponding adjective.
Snabb quick
Hon går snabbt. She walks quickly.

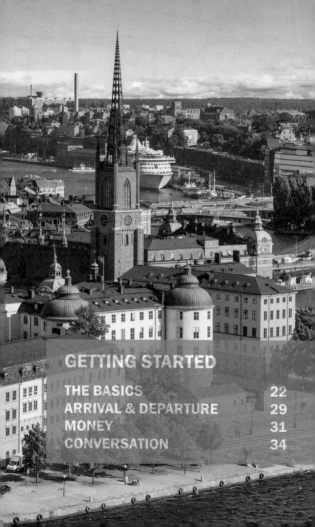

GETTING STARTED

THE BASICS

NUMBERS

0	**noll** *nohl*
1	**ett** *eht*
2	**två** *tvoa*
3	**tre** *tree*
4	**fyra** <u>*few*</u> • *ra*
5	**fem** *fehm*
6	**sex** *sehx*
7	**sju** *sheu*
8	**åtta** *oh* • <u>*ta*</u>
9	**nio** <u>*nee*</u> • *oa*
10	**tio** <u>*tee*</u> • *oa*
11	**elva** <u>*ehl*</u> • *va*
12	**tolv** *tohlv*
13	**tretton** <u>*treh*</u> • *tohn*
14	**fjorton** <u>*fyeur*</u> • *tohn*
15	**femton** <u>*fehm*</u> • *tohn*

16	**sexton** <u>sehx</u> • tohn	
17	**sjutton** <u>sheu</u> • tohn	
18	**arton** <u>ar</u> • tohn	
19	**nitton** <u>nih</u> • tohn	
20	**tjugo** <u>shcheu</u> • goa	
21	**tjugoett** <u>shcheu</u> • goa • eht	
22	**tjugotvå** <u>shcheu</u> • goa • tvoa	
30	**trettio** <u>treh</u> • tee • oa	
31	**trettioett** <u>treh</u> • tee • oa • eht	
40	**fyrtio** <u>fuhr</u> • tee • oa	
50	**femtio** <u>fehm</u> • tee • oa	
60	**sextio** <u>sehx</u> • tee • oa	
70	**sjuttio** <u>sheu</u> • tee • oa	
80	**åttio** <u>oh</u> • tee • oa	
90	**nittio** <u>nih</u> • tee • oa	
100	**hundra** <u>huhn</u> • dra	
101	**hundraett** <u>huhn</u> • dra • eht	
200	**två hundra** <u>tvoa</u> huhn • dra	
500	**fem hundra** <u>fehm</u> huhn • dra	
1,000	**ett tusen** eht <u>teu</u> • sehn	
10,000	**tio tusen** <u>tee</u> • oa <u>teu</u> • sehn	
1,000,000	**en miljon** ehn mihl • <u>yoan</u>	

ORDINAL NUMBERS

first	**första**
	<u>furs</u> • ta
second	**andra**
	<u>an</u> • dra
third	**tredje**
	<u>tree</u> • dyer

fourth	**fjärde**
	fyair • der
fifth	**femte**
	fehm • ter
once	**en gång**
	ehn goang
twice	**två gånger**
	tvoa goang • ehr
three times	**tre gånger**
	tree goang • ehr

TIME

NEED TO KNOW

What time is it?	**Hur mycket är klockan?**
	heur mew • ker air kloh • kan
It's noon [midday].	**Klockan är tolv.**
	kloh • kan air tolv
Midnight.	**Midnatt.**
	meed • nat
From 9 o'clock to 5 o'clock.	**Från nio till sjutton.**
	froan nee • oa tihl sheu • tohn
It's twenty after [past] four.	**Den är tjugo över fyra.**
	dehn air shcheu • goa ur • ver few • ra
It's a quarter to nine.	**Den är kvart i nio.**
	dehn air kvart ee nee • oa
5:30 a.m.	**Halv sex på morgonen.**
	halv sehx poa mor • oh • nehn
5:30 p.m.	**Halv sex på kvällen.**
	halv sehx poa kveh • lehn

Sweden officially follows the 24-hour clock. Formal communication, such as public transporation schedules and TV programming, follows this system. However, in ordinary conversation, time is generally expressed as shown above, often with the addition of **på morgonen** (in the morning), **på förmiddagen** (mid-morning), **på eftermiddagen** (in the afternoon), **på kvällen** (in the evening) and **på natten** (at night).

DAYS

NEED TO KNOW

Monday	**måndag**
	moan • dahg
Tuesday	**tisdag**
	tees • dahg
Wednesday	**onsdag**
	oans • dahg
Thursday	**torsdag**
	toash • dahg
Friday	**fredag**
	free • dahg
Saturday	**lördag**
	lurr • dahg
Sunday	**söndag**
	surn • dahg

DATES

yesterday	**igår**
	ee • goar
today	**idag**
	ee • dahg
tomorrow	**imorgon**
	ee • mo • ron
day	**dag**
	dahg
week	**vecka**
	veh • ka
month	**månad**
	moa • nad
year	**år**
	oar

MONTHS

January	**januari**
	ya • neu • ah • ree
February	**februari**
	fehb • reu • ah • ree
March	**mars**
	mash
April	**april**
	ap • rihl
May	**maj**
	maiy
June	**juni**
	yeu • nee
July	**juli**
	yeu • lee

August	**augusti**
	a • guhss • tee
September	**september**
	sehp • tehm • behr
October	**oktober**
	ohk • toa • behr
November	**november**
	noh • vehm • behr
December	**december**
	dee • sehm • behr

(i)

Sweden follows a day-month-year format instead of
the month-day-year format used in the U.S.
E.g.: July 25, 2008; **25/07/08** = 7/25/2008 in the U.S.

SEASONS

spring	**vår**
	voar
summer	**sommar**
	soh • mar
fall [autumn]	**höst**
	huhst
winter	**vinter**
	vihn • tehr

HOLIDAYS

January 1: **Nyårsdagen** New Year's Day
January 6: **Trettondagen** Epiphany
May 1: **Första maj** May Day
June 6: **Flaggans dag** Flag Day

December 25: **Juldagen** Christmas Day
December 26: **Annandag jul** Boxing Day
Moveable dates include:
Långfredagen Good Friday
Kristi himmelfärdsdag Ascension
Pingstdagen Whitsunday
Allhelgonadagen All Saints' Day
Midsommardagen Midsummer Day

The two most important holidays in Sweden are Midsummer and Christmas. **Midsommardagen** (Midsummer) is celebrated with midsummer poles (similar to the may pole) and traditional songs and dances. Traditional food includes **matjesill** (pickled herring), fresh fish and schnapps. For **Juldagen** (Christmas), special cakes and other delicious treats are prepared, such as **pepparkakor** (ginger cookies), **saffranbullar** (saffron buns) and **julbord** (Christmas **smörgåsbord,** a festive buffet). Though not an official holiday, **Luciadagen** (St. Lucia Day) on December 13 marks the beginning of the Chirstmas season. Swedes also celebrate the beginning of spring on April 30, which is known as **Valborgsmässoafton,** with huge bonfires, fireworks and singing. June 6 is **Flaggans dag** (Flag Day), the national day of Sweden. Streets are decorated with yellow and blue, the colors of the Swedish flag, patriotic speeches are made and traditional games and meals are enjoyed.

ARRIVAL & DEPARTURE

NEED TO KNOW

I'm here on vacation [holiday]/business.

Jag är här på semester/affärsresa.
Yahg air hair poa seh • mehs • ter/ a • fairs • ree • sa

I'm going to…

Jag ska resa till...
yahg skah ree • sa tihl...

I'm staying at a hotel/youth hostel.

Jag bor på hotell/vandrarhem.
yahg boar poa hoh • tehl/ vahnd • rar • hehm

BORDER CONTROL

I'm just passing through.

Jag är bara på genomresa.
yahg air bah • ra poa ye • nohm • ree • sa

I would like to declare…

Jag skulle vilja förtulla...
yahg skuh • ler vihl • ya furr • tuh • la...

I have nothing to declare.

Jag har inget att förtulla.
yahg hahr ihng • eht at furr • tuh • la

YOU MAY HEAR...

Er biljett/Ert pass, tack.
eer bihl • yeht/ eert pas tak

Your ticket/
passport,
please.

Vad är syftet med ert besök?
vahd air sewf • tet meed ehrt beh • surk

What's the
purpose of your
visit?

Var bor du?
vahr boar deu

Where are you
staying?

Hur länge ska du stanna?
heur lehng • er skah deu stan • a

How long are
you staying?

Vem är du här med?
vehm air deu hair meed

Who are you
here with?

Metta le iniziali/Firmi qui.
*meht • tah leh ee • nee • tsyah • lee/
feer • mee kwee*

Initial/Sign
here.

YOU MAY SEE...

TULL	customs
TAXFRIA VAROR	duty-free goods
VAROR ATT FÖRTULLA	goods to declare
INGET ATT FÖRTULLA	nothing to declare
PASSKONTROLL	passport control
POLIS	police

YOU MAY HEAR...

Har du något att förtulla?
hahr deu noa • goht at furr • tuh • la

Anything to declare?

Du måste betala tull för det här.
deu mos • ter beh • tah • la tuhl furr dee hair

You must pay duty on this.

Var snäll och öppna den här väskan.
vahr snehl ohk urp • na dehn hair vehs • kan

Please open this bag.

MONEY

NEED TO KNOW

Where's...?	**Var ligger...?**
	vahr lih • gehr...
the ATM	**bankomaten**
	bank • oa • mah • tehn
the bank	**banken**
	bank • ehn
the currency exchange office	**växelkontoret**
	vehx • ehl • kohn • toar • eht
What time does the bank open/close?	**När öppnar/stänger banken?**
	nair urp • nahr/stehng • ehr bank • ehn
I'd like to change dollars/pounds into kronor.	**Jag skulle vilja växla dollar/pund till kronor.**
	yahg skuh • ler vihl • ya vehx • la doh • lar/pund tihl kroa • nohr
I want to cash some traveler's checks [cheques].	**Jag skulle vilja lösa in några resecheckar.**
	yahg skuh • ler vihl • yalur • sa ihn noa • gra ree • seh • sheh • kar

AT THE BANK

Can I exchange foreign currency here?
Kan jag växla pengar här?
kan yahg <u>vehx</u> • la <u>pehng</u> • ar hair

What's the exchange rate?
Vad är växelkursen?
vahd air <u>vehx</u> • ehl • keur • shehn

I think there's a mistake.
Jag tror det är ett misstag.
Yahg troar dee air eht mis • tagh

How much is the fee?
Hur mycket är expeditionsavgiften?
Heur <u>mew</u> • ker air ehx • peh • dee • <u>shoa</u>ns • afv <u>yihf</u> • tehn

I've lost my traveler's checks.
Jag har tappat mina resecheckar.
Yahg hahr <u>ta</u> • pat <u>mee</u> • na <u>ree</u> • seh • sheh • kar

I've lost my card.
Jag har tappat mitt kort.
yahg hahr <u>ta</u> • pat miht koart

My credit cards have been stolen.
Mina kreditkort är stulna.
<u>mee</u> • na kreh • <u>deet</u> • koart air <u>steul</u> • na

My card doesn't work.
Mitt kort fungerar inte.
miht koart fuhn • <u>gee</u> • rar ihn • ter

The ATM ate my card.
Uttagsautomaten tog mitt kort.
eut • tahgs • ah • toa • mah • tehn toagh miht koart.

For Numbers, see page 22.

YOU MAY SEE...

SÄTT IN KORTET	insert card
AVBESTÄLLA	cancel
RENSA	clear
ENTER	enter
PINKOD	PIN
TA UT	withdraw
FRÅN CHEKKONTO	from checking [current] account
FRÅN SPARKONTO	from savings account
KVITTOT	receipt

Cash can be obtained from a **Bankomat** (ATM) with MasterCard, Visa, Eurocard, American Express and other international credit cards or with a debit card. It is also possible to exchange traveler's checks in Sweden. In recent years, it has become quite common for the banks to refer customers with traveler's checks to the nearest **växelkontor** (currency exchange business) such as Forex or X-Change. These businesses are often located near or in points of departure/arrival such as airports or train stations, but can also be found in city centers. Remember to bring your passport with you for identification when you want to exchange money or cash traveler's checks. Most banks close at 3:00 p.m., though some are open later one day a week, often on Thursdays.

YOU MAY SEE...

Unlike the majority of other European Union countries,
Sweden has not adopted the euro as its national currency.
Sweden's monetary unit is the **krona** (singular) or **kronor**
(plural) abbreviated to **SEK**.
The **krona** is divided into **öre**.
Coins: 50 **öre**, 1 **krona**, 5 and 10 **kronor**
Banknotes: 20, 50, 100, 500 and 1000 **kronor**

CONVERSATION

NEED TO KNOW

Hello!	**Hej!**
	hay
How are you?	**Hur står det till?**
	heur stoar dee tihl
Fine, thanks.	**Bra, tack. Och du?**
And you?	*brah tak ohk deu*
Excuse me!	**Ursäkta!**
	eur • shehk • ta
Do you speak	**Talar du engelska?**
English?	*tah • lar deu ehng • ehl • ska*
What's your name?	**Vad heter du?**
	vahd hee • tehr deu
My name is...	**Jag heter...**
	yahg hee • tehr...

Nice to meet you.	**Trevligt att träffas.**
	treev • lihgt at _trehf_ • as.
Where are you from?	**Var kommer du ifrån?**
	vahr _ko_ • mehr deu ee • _froan_
I'm from the U.S./U.K.	**Jag kommer från USA/ Storbritannien.**
	yahg _koh_ • mehr froan eu ehs ah/ _stoap_ • bree • _tan_ • yehn
What do you do?	**Vad sysslar du med?**
	vahd _sews_ • lar deu meed
I work for…	**Jag jobbar på.**
	yahg _yohb_ • ar poa…
I'm a student.	**Jag är student.**
	yahg air _stuh_ • dent
I'm retired.	**Jag är pensionär.**
	yahg air pang • shoa • _nair_
Do you like…?	**Tycker du om…?**
	tew • kehr deu ohm…
Goodbye.	**Hej då.**
	hay • doa
See you later.	**Vi ses.**
	vee sees

LANGUAGE DIFFICULTIES

Do you speak English?	**Talar du engelska?** _tah • lar deu ehng • ehl • ska_
Does anyone here speak English?	**Talar någon engelska här?** _tah • lar noa • gohn ehng • ehl • ska hair_
I don't speak Swedish.	**Jag talar inte svenska.** _yahg tah • lar ihn • ter svehn • ska_
Could you speak more slowly?	**Kan du tala lite långsammare?** _kan deu tah • la lee • ter loang • sam • a • rer_
Could you repeat that?	**Kan du upprepa det?** _kan deu uhp • ree • pah dee_
Excuse me?	**Ursäkta?** _eur • shehk • ta_
What was that?	**Vad var det?** _vahd vahr dee_
Can you spell it?	**Kan du stava det?** _kahn deu stah • va deht_
Write it down, please.	**Skriv ner det, tack.** _skreev neer dee tak_
Can you translate this for me?	**Kan du översätta det här?** _kan deu ur • ver • seh • ta deet hair_
What does this/that mean?	**Vad betyder det här/där?** _vad beh • tew • der dee hair/dair_
I understand.	**Jag förstår.** _yahg furr • stoar_
I don't understand.	**Jag förstår inte.** _yahg furr • stoar ihn • ter_
Do you understand?	**Förstår du?** _furr • stoar deu_

YOU MAY HEAR...

Jag talar bara lite engelska.
yahg tah•lar bah•ra lee•ter ehng•ehl•ska

I speak only a little English.

Jag talar inte engelska.
yahg tah•lar in•ter ehng•ehl•ska

I don't speak English.

Swedes shake hands when greeting someone and when saying goodbye; this applies for meeting new people but is also often the case with colleagues or acquaintances. When you meet someone for the first time, shake hands and give your name. As in many countries, titles are more commonly used by the older generation, but you will sometimes hear **herr** (Mr.), **fru** (Mrs.) and **fröken** (Miss) used, as well as professional titles, e.g., **doktor** (doctor), **ingenjör** (engineer), etc.

MAKING FRIENDS

Hello.	**Hej.**
	hay
Good morning.	**God morgon.**
	goad mor•on
Good afternoon.	**God middag.**
	goad mi•dahg
Good evening.	**God afton.**
	goad af•tohn
My name is...	**Jag heter...**
	yahg hee•tehr...

What's your name?	**Vad heter du?**
	vahd hee • tehr deu
I'd like to introduce you to...	**Får jag presentera...**
	foar yahg preh • sehn • tee • ra...
Pleased to meet you.	**Trevligt att träffas.**
	treev • lihgt at treh • fas
How are you?	**Hur står det till?**
	heur stoar dee tihl
Fine, thanks.	**Bra, tack.**
	brah tak
And you?	**Och du?**
	ohk deu

TRAVEL TALK

I'm here...	**Jag är här...**
	yahg air hair...
on business	**på affärsresa**
	poa a • fairs • ree • sa
on vacation [holiday]	**på semester**
	poa seh • mehs • tehr
studying	**för studier**
	furr steu • de • ehr
I'm staying for...	**Jag ska stanna i...**
	yahg skah sta • na ee...
I've been here..	**Jag har varit här i...**
	yahg hahr vah • riht hair ee...
a day	**en dag**
	ehn dahg
a week	**en vecka**
	ehn veh • ka
a month	**en månad**
	ehn moa • nad
Where are you from?	**Var kommer du ifrån?**
	vahr koh • mehr deu ee • froan

I'm from.	**Jag kommer från.**
	yahg koh • mehr froan…

For Numbers, see page 22.

PERSONAL

Who are you here with?	**Vem är du här med?**
	vehm air deu hair meed
I'm on my own.	**Jag är ensam.**
	yahg air ehn • sam
I'm with…	**Jag är här med…**
	yahg air hair meed…
my husband/wife	**min man/fru**
	mihn man/freu
my boyfriend	**min pojkvän**
	mihn povk • vehn
girlfriend	**flickvän**
	flihk • vehn
a friend/friends	**en vän/vänner**
	ehn vehn/venhn • ehr
a colleague	**en kollega**
	ehn koh • lee • ga/
colleagues	**kolleger**
	koh • lee • goahr
When's your birthday?	**När fyller du år?**
	nair fewl • ehr deu oar
How old are you?	**Hur gammal är du?**
	heur gah • mal air deu
I'm…	**Jag är…**
	yahg air…
single	**ogift**
	oa • yift
in a relationship	**i ett förhållande**
	ee eht furr • hoal • an • der

engaged	**förlovad**
	fuhr • loh • vad
married	**gift**
	yihft
divorced	**skild**
	shihld
separated	**separerad**
	seh • pa • ree • rad
I'm a widow/ widower.	**Jag är änka/änkling.**
	yahg air ehng • ka/ehnak • lihna
Do you have children/ grandchildren?	**Har du barn/barnbarn?**
	hahr deu bahrn/bahrn • bahrn

For Numbers, see page 22.

WORK & SCHOOL

What do you do?	**Vad sysslar du med?**
	vahd sews • lar deu meed
What are you studying?	**Vad läser du?**
	vahd lai • sehr deu
I'm studying…	**Jag läser…**
	yahg lai • sehr…
I work full time/ part time.	**Jag arbetar heltid/deltid.**
	yahg ahr • beh • tar hehl • teed/ dehl • teed
I work at home.	**Jag arbetar hemifrån.**
	yahg ahr • beh • tar hehm • ih • froan
I'm unemployed.	**Jag är arbetslös.**
	yahg air ar • behts • lus
Who do you work for?	**Vilken firma jobbar du på?**
	vihl • kehn fihr • ma yohb • ar deu poa
I work for…	**Jag jobbar på…**
	yahg yohb • ar poa…
Here's my business card.	**Här är mitt kort.**
	hair air miht koahrt

WEATHER

What's the weather forecast for tomorrow?	**Vad är väderleksrapporten för imorgon?**	
	vahd air vair • dehr • leeks • ra • pohr • tehn furr ee • mo • ron	
What beautiful/ terrible weather!	**Vilket vackert/förskräckligt väder!**	
	vihl • keht va • kert/furr • skrehk • ligt vair • dehr	
It's…	**Det är…**	
	dee air…	
hot/cold	**varmt/kallt**	
	varmt/kahlt	
cool/warm	**svalt/varmt**	
	svahlt/varmt	
rainy/sunny	**regnigt/soligt**	
	rehng • nihkt/soal • ikt	
snowy/icy	**snöigt/halt**	
	snur • ikt/hahlt	
Do I need a jacket/ an umbrella?	**Behöver jag en jacka/ett paraply?**	
	beh • hur • ver yahg ehn yah • ka/eht pa • ra • plew	

EXPLORING

GETTING AROUND

NEED TO KNOW

How do I get to town?	**Hur kommer jag till staden?**
	heur koh • mehr yahg tihl stahd • ehn
Where is...?	**Var ligger...?**
	vahr lih • gehr...
the airport	**flygplatsen**
	flewg • plats • ehn
the train [railway] station	**järnvägsstationen**
	yairn • vehgs • sta • shoa • nehn
the bus station	**bussterminalen**
	bus • tehr • mee • nah • lehn
the subway [underground] station	**tunnelbanestationen**
	teu • nehl • bah • neh • sta • shoan • ehn
How far is it?	**Hur långt är det?**
	heur loangt air dee
Where can I buy tickets?	**Var kan jag köpa biljetter?**
	vahr kan yahg chur • pa bil • yeht • tehr

A one-way [single]/ round-trip [return].	**Enkel./Retur.** *ehng • kehl/reh • teur*
How much does it cost?	**Hur mycket kostar det?** *heur mew • ker kos • tar dee*
Are there any discounts?	**Finns det några rabatter?** *fihns dee noa • gra ra • bat • ehr*
Which gate?	**Vid vilken gate?** *veed vihl • kehn gayt*
Which line?	**Vilken kö?** *vihl • kehn kur*
Which platform?	**Vilken plattform?** *vihl • kehn plat • fohrm*
Where can I get a taxi?	**Var kan jag få tag på en taxi?** *vahr kan yahg foa tahg poa ehn tax • ee*
Please take me to this address.	**Var snäll och kör mig till denna address.** *vahr snehl ohk churr may tihl deh • na ad • rehs*
Where can I rent a car?	**Var kan jag hyra en bil?** *vahr kan yahg hew • ra ehn beel*
I'd like a map.	**Jag skulle vilja ha en karta.** *Yahg skuh • ler vihl • ya hah ehn kahr • ta*

TICKETS

When is…to	**När går…till Uppsala?** *nair goar…tihl uhp • sah • la Uppsala?*
the (first) bus	**(första) bussen** *(furs • ta) buhs • ehn*

the (next) flight	**(nästa) flyg**
	(nehs • ta) flewg
the (last) train	**(sista) tåget**
	(sihs • ta) toa • geht
Where can I buy tickets?	**Var kan jag köpa biljetter?**
	vahr kan yahg chur • pa bihl • yeht • er
One ticket/Two tickets, please.	**En biljett/Två biljetter, tack.**
	ehn bil • yet/tvoa bil • yeht • er tak
For today/tomorrow.	**Till dagens/imorgon.**
	tihl dah • gens/ee • mo • ron
...ticket.	**...biljett.**
	...bihl • yeht
A one-way [single]	**En enkel**
	ehn ehng • kehl
A return-trip	**En retur**
	ehn reh • teur
A first class	**En första klass**
	ehn furr • sta klas
A business class	**En i affärsklass**
	Ehn ee a • fairs • klas
An economy class	**En turist klass**
	ehn tuh • rihst klas
How much does it cost?	**Hur mycket kostar det?**
	heur mew • ker kos • tar dee
Is there a discount for...?	**Blir det rabatt för...?**
	bleer dee ra • bat furr...
children	**barn**
	bahrn
students	**studerande**
	steu • dee • ran • der
senior citizens	**pensionärer**
	pan • shoa • nair • ehr
tourists	**turister**
	tuh • rihst • ehr

The express bus/ express train, please.	**Expressbussen/expresståget, tack.** *Ehx•prehs•buhs•ehn/ ehx•prehs•toa•geht, tak*
The local bus/train, please.	**Lokalbussen/tåget, tack.** *Loh•kahl•buhs•en/toa•geht, tak*
I have an e-ticket.	**Jag har en e-biljett.** *yahg hahr ehn ee•bihl•<u>yet</u>*
Can I buy a ticket on the bus/train?	**Kan jag köpa en biljett på bussen/ tåget?** *kan yahg <u>chur</u>•pa ehn bihl•<u>yeht</u> poa bus•ehn/<u>toa</u>•geht*
Do I have to stamp the ticket before boarding?	**Ska jag stämpla biljetten innan jag går ombord?** *Skah yahg stehm•pla bil•yet•ehn•ihn•ahn•yahg•goar• ohm•bohrd*
How long is this ticket valid?	**Hur länge gäller denna biljett?** *Heur lehng•er yeh•lehr deh•na bihl•yet*
Can I return on the same ticket?	**Kan jag åka tillbaka med samma biljett?** *Kahn yahg oak•ha tihl•bah•ka mehd sam•a bihl•yet*
I'd like to…my reservation.	**Jag skulle vilja…min bokning.** *Yahg <u>skuh</u>•ler vihl•ya…mihn <u>boak</u>•nihng*
cancel	**avbeställa** *<u>afv</u>•beh•steh•la*
change	**ändra** *<u>ehn</u>•dra*
confirm	**bekräfta** *beh•<u>krehf</u>•ta*

AIRPORT TRANSFER

How much is a taxi to the airport?	**Vad kostar en taxi till flygplatsen?** *Vahd kos•tar ehn tax•ee tihl flewg•plat•sehn*
To…Airport, please.	**Till…Flygplats, tack.** *tihl…flewg•plats tak*
My airline is…	**Mitt flygbolag är…** *miht flewg•boa•lahg air…*
My flight leaves at…	**Mitt flyg avgår klockan…** *miht flewg afv•goar kloh•kan…*
I'm in a rush.	**Jag har bråttom.** *yahg hahr broa•tohm*
Can you take an alternate route?	**Kan du köra någon annan väg?** *kan deu chur•ra noa•gohn an•nan vehg*
Can you drive faster/slower?	**Kan du köra lite fortare/långsammare?** *kan deu chur•ra lee•ter foar•ta•rer/loang•sam•a•rer*

YOU MAY HEAR…

Vilket flygbolag reser du med?
vihl•keht flewg•boa•lahg ree•sehr deu meed

What airline are you flying?

Inrikes eller utrikes?
in•ree•kehs ehl•er eut•ree•kehs

Domestic or International?

Vilken terminal?
vihl•kehn tehr•mee•nahl

What terminal?

CHECKING IN

Where is check-in?	**Var är incheckningen?**
	vahr air in • shehk • nihng • ehn
My name is...	**Jag heter...**
	yahg hee • ter...
I'm going to...	**Jag ska resa till...**
	yahg skah ree • sa tihl...
I have...	**Jag har....**
	Yahg hahr...
one suitcase	**en resväska**
	ehn rehs • vehs • ka
two suitcases	**två resväskor**
	tvoh rehs • vehs • kohr
one piece of	**ett handbagage**
hand luggage	*eht hand • ba • gah • sh*
How much luggage	**Hur mycket gratis bagage får man ha?**
is allowed?	*heur mew • ker grah • tihs ba • goash foar man hah*
Is that pounds	**Är det i pund eller kilo?**
or kilos?	*Air deht ee pund ehl • er cheeh • loh*
Which terminal/	**Vid vilken terminal/gate går**
gate does flight...	**flygnummer...?**
leave from?	*veed vihl • kehn tehr • mee • nahl/gayt goar flewg • nuhm • ehr...*
I'd like a window/	**Jag skulle vilja ha en fönsterplats/**
an aisle seat.	**plats i mittgången.**
	yahg skuh • ler vihl • ya hah ehn furns • tehr • plats/plats ee miht • goang • ehn
When do we leave/	**När avgår vi/är vi framme?**
arrive?	*nair afv • goar vee/air vee fra • mer*

Is flight...delayed?	**Är det någon försening på flyg...?**
	*air d**ee** <u>noa</u> • gohn furr • <u>seen</u> • ihng p**oa***
	flewg...
How late will it be?	**Hur försenat är det?**
	*heur furr • <u>seen</u> • at air d**ee***

YOU MAY SEE...

ANKOMST	arrivals
AVGÅNG	departures
BAGAGEUTLÄMNING	baggage claim
INRIKESFLYG	domestic flights
UTRIKESFLYG	international flights
CHECKA IN	check-in
CHECKA IN E-BILJETT	e-ticket check-in
AVGÅNGSGATER	departure gates

YOU MAY HEAR...

Nästa!
nehs • ta

Next!

Er biljett/Ert pass, tack.
eer bihl • yet/ eert pas tak

Your ticket/ passport, please.

Hur mycket bagage har du?
heur mew • ker ba • goash hahr deu

How much luggage do you have?

Du har övervikt.
deu hahr ur • vehr • vikt

You have excess luggage.

Det där är för tungt/för stort handbagage.
dee dair air furr teungt/furr stoart hand • ba • goash

That's too heavy/large for a carry-on [to carry on board].

Packade du väskorna själv?
pa • ka • der deu vehs • kohr • na shehlv

Did you pack these bags yourself?

Har någon gett er något att ta med?
hahr noa • gohn yeht eer noa • goht at tah meed

Did anyone give you anything to carry?

Töm era fickor, tack.
turm ee • ra fihk • ohr tak

Empty your pockets, please.

Ta av er skorna, tack.
ta afv eer skoar • na tak

Take off your shoes, please.

Nu är ni välkommna att borda flight nummer...
neu air nee vail • kohm • na at bohr • da flajt nuhm • ehr...

Now boarding flight...

LUGGAGE

Where is/are...?	**Var finns...?**
	vahr fihns...
the luggage carts [trolleys]	**bagagekärrorna**
	ba • goash • chair • ohr • na
the luggage lockers	**förvaringsskåpen**
	furr • vah • rihng • skoap • ehn
the baggage claim	**bagageutlämningen**
	ba • goash • eut • lehm • nihng • ehn
I've lost my baggage.	**Jag har förlorat mitt bagage.**
	yahg hahr furr • loa • rat miht ba • goash
My baggage has been stolen.	**Mitt bagage har blivit stulet.**
	miht ba • goash hahr blee • viht steu • leht
My suitcase was damaged.	**Min resväska blev skadad.**
	Mihn rees • vehs • ka bleev skah • dad

FINDING YOUR WAY

Where is...?	**Var finns...?**
	vahr fihns...
the currency exchange office	**växelkontoret**
	vehx • ehl • kohn • toar • eht
the car hire	**biluthyrningen**
	beel • eut • hewr • nihng • ehn
the exit	**utgången**
	eut • goang • ehn
the taxi	**taxin**
	tax • een
Is there...into town?	**Finns det...in till stan?**
	fihns dee...ihn tihl stahn
a bus	**en buss**
	ehn buhs

a train	**ett tåg**
	eht t**o**ag
a subway	**tunnelbana**
	<u>tuh</u> • nehl • bah • na

For Asking Directions, see page 64.

YOU MAY SEE... 👁

PLATTFORM	platform
SPÅR	tracks
INFORMATION	information
BILJETTKONTOR	ticket office
ANKOMST	arrival
AVGÅNG	departure

TRAIN

How do I get to the train station?	**Hur kommer jag till järnvägsstationen?**
	heur <u>koh</u> • mehr yahg tihl
	<u>yairn</u> • vaigs • sta • <u>shoa</u> • nehn
How far is it?	**Hur långt är det?**
	*heur l**o**angt air d**ee***
Where is/are...?	**Var finns...?**
	vahr fihns...
the ticket office	**biljettkontoret**
	bihl • <u>yet</u> • kohn • <u>toar</u> • eht
the luggage lockers	**förvaringsskåpen**
	*furr • <u>vah</u> • rihng • sk**o**ap • ehn*
the platforms	**plattformarna**
	<u>plat</u> • fohr • mar • na
Could I have a schedule [timetable], please?	**Kan jag få en tidtabell, tack?**
	*kan yahg f**o**a ehn <u>teed</u> • ta • <u>behl</u> tak*

How long is the trip?	**Hur lång tid tar resan?**
	heur loang teed tahr ree•san
Is it a direct train?	**Är det ett direkttåg?**
	air deh•ta eht dihr•ekt•toag
Do I have to change trains?	**Behöver jag byta tåg?**
	beh•hur•vehr yahg bew•ta toag
Is the train on time?	**Är tåget i tid?**
	air toag•het ee tihd

For Time, see page 24.

(i)

Statens järnvägar or **SJ** (the Swedish State Railway) operates an extensive network covering the entire country, while also offering international connections to Oslo, Copenhagen and Berlin. The X2000 train, which reaches speeds up to 200 km/h, serves many of Sweden's greater cities and towns. Long-distance trains have restaurant cars and/or buffets, and there are also sleepers and couchettes for both first and second class. The system is reliable and comfortable, and offers a wide range of travel options with respect to schedule and cost. Discount tickets are available for young children, families, students and senior citizens. Special travel cards and programs are also available. On some trains, marked **R** or **IC**, you must reserve a seat by purchasing a **sittplatsbiljett** in addition to your travel ticket. For extraordinary scenery, try the northern **Inlandsbanan** (Inland Railway) service, which runs from Mora in Dalarna to Gällivare beyond the Arctic circle. The **Vildmarksexpressen** (Wilderness Express) has old 1930s coaches and a gourmet restaurant, and runs on the same line between Östersund and Gällivare, with stops and excursions.

DEPARTURES

Which platform does the train to…leave from?	**Vilken plattform går tåget till…från?** *Vihl • kehn plat • fohrm goar tao • geht froan*
When is the train to…?	**När går tåget till…?** *nair goar toa • geht tihl…*
Is this the right platform for…?	**Är det här rätta plattformen till…?** *air dee hair reh • ta plat • fohr • mehn tihl…*
Where is platform…?	**Var är plattform…?** *vahr air plat • fohrm…*
Where do I change for…?	**Var måste jag byta till…?** *vahr mos • ter yahg bew • ta tihl…*

ON BOARD

Can I sit here/open the window?	**Kan jag sitta här/öppna fönstret?** *Kan yahg sihta hair/urp • na fuhns • streht*
Is this seat taken?	**Är den här platsen upptagen?** *air dehn hair plats • ehn uhp • tah • gehn*
That's my seat.	**Det där är min plats.** *dee dair air mihn plats*
Here's my reservation.	**Här är min bokning** *Hair air meen boak • nihng*

BUS

Where's the bus station?	**Var är bussterminalen?** *vahr air bus • tehr • mih • nahl • ehn*
How far is it?	**Hur långt är det?** *heur loangt air dee*
How do I get to…?	**Hur kommer jag till…?** *heur koh • mehr yahg tihl…*

Does the bus stop at…?	**Stannar bussen vid…?** _stan • ar_ _buhs_ • en veed…
Could you tell me when to get off?	**Kan du tala om för mig när jag ska stiga av?** kan deu _tah_ • la ohm _furr_ may nair yahg skah _stee_ • ga afv
Do I have to change buses?	**Behöver jag byta buss?** beh • _hur_ • vehr yahg _bew_ • ta buhs
Stop here, please.	**Stanna här, tack.** _sta_ • na hair tak

For Tickets, see page 45.

YOU MAY HEAR…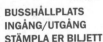

Påstigning!
 poa • steeg • nihng

All aboard!

Biljetter, tack.
 bihl • _yet_ • er tak

Tickets, please.

Du måste byta i…
 deu _moss_ • ter _bew_ • ta ee…

You have to change in…

Nästa hållplats…
 nehs • ta _hoal_ • plats…

Next stop…

YOU MAY SEE…

BUSSHÅLLPLATS	bus stop
INGÅNG/UTGÅNG	enter/exit
STÄMPLA ER BILJETT	stamp your ticket

ⓘ

Public transportation in Sweden is an excellent and
well-maintained system that includes **bussar** (buses),
tunnelbanan (subways), **spårvagnar** (trams) and **tåg**
(trains). All of these run frequently, usually between
5:00 a.m. and midnight on weekdays and a bit later on
weekends. Most cities and towns have a bus system,
though only a few have trams and subways. While it
is possible to purchase single tickets for the different
modes of public transportation, it is more cost efficient to
purchase a card or set of tickets if you are going to be using
a particular network frequently. Most major cities have
websites that provide up to date information on routes,
tickets and prices; many of the sites have English as a
language option.

SUBWAY

Where's the nearest subway [underground] station?	**Var är närmaste tunnelbanestation?** *Vahr air <u>nair</u> • mas • ter* *tuh • nehl • bah • neh • sta • <u>shoan</u>*
Which direction?	**Åt vilket håll?** *Oat vihl • keht hohl*
Can I have a map of the subway [underground], please?	**Kan jag få en tunnelbanekarta, tack?** *Kan yahg foa ehn* *tuh • nehl • bah • neh • <u>kahr</u> • ta tak*
Which line should I take for…?	**Vilken linje ska jag ta till…?** *vihl • kehn <u>leen</u> • yeh skah yahg tah tihl…*
Where do I change for…?	**Var måste jag byta till…?** *vahr <u>mos</u> • ter yahg <u>bew</u> • ta tihl…*

Is this the train to…?	**Är det här tåget till…?**
	air dee hair <u>toa</u> • geht tihl…
How many stops to…?	**Hur många hållplatser är det till…?**
	Heur moh • ngah hohl • plat • sehr air deht tihl…
Where are we?	**Var är vi?**
	vahr air vee

For Tickets, see page 45.

ⓘ

The subway in Stockholm is efficient and easy to use. It runs from 5:00 a.m. to midnight on weekdays. Tickets are valid for one hour from the time they are stamped and can be bought from ticket booths; discount cards can be purchased from **Pressbyrån** (a newsstand). Tickets can also be purchased at **SL Centers**, some tourist offices and certain grocery stores. The public transportation websites will have information on these retailers and businesses and what types of tickets they sell. Day and multi-day cards are also available. Subway and bus tickets in Stockholm are interchangeable.

👁

YOU MAY SEE…

LIVBÅT	life boat
FLYTVÄST	life jacket
ACTIVERA HANDBROMSEN	use parking brake
LÄMNA INTE VÄRDESAKER I BILEN	do not leave valuables in your car

BOAT & FERRY

When is the car ferry to Gotland leaving?	**Hur dags går bilfärjan till Gotland?** *heur daks goar beel•fair•yan tihl goht•land*
Where are the life jackets?	**Var finns flytvästarna?** *vahr fihns flewt•vehs•tar•na*
Can I take my car?	**Kan jag ta med min bil?** *Kahn yahg tah mehd meen bihl*
Can I drive on to the ferry now?	**Får jag köra ombord nu?** *foar yahg chur•ra ohm bohrd neu*
What time is the next sailing?	**Hur dags går nästa?** *Heur daks goar nehs•ta*
Can I book a seat/cabin?	**Kan jag boka en plats/hytt?** *Kahn yahg boa•ka plats/hewt*
How long is the trip?	**Hur lång är resan?** *heur loang air ree•san*
Where should I park?	**Var ska jag parkera?** *vahr skah yahg par•kee•ra*

ⓘ

Regular boat and ferry services, carrying cars and passengers, link Sweden to neighboring countries such as Norway, Denmark and Germany as well as to the U.K. Ferry services from Stockholm to the vacation destinations of Åland and Gotland in the Baltic Sea are very popular, as are ferries to Finland, Estonia and Latvia. Not to be missed are the ferry and steamer trips from Stockholm to the many surrounding islands, known as **Skärgården** (the Archipelago).

TAXI

Where can I get a taxi?	**Var kan jag få tag på en taxi?** *vahr kan yahg foa tahg poa ehn tax•ee*
I'd like a taxi now/for tomorrow at…	**Jag skulle vilja ha en taxi nu/imorgon klockan…** *yahg skuh•ler vihl•ya hah ehn tax•ee neu/ee•mo•ron kloh•kan…*
Can you send a taxi?	**Kan du skicka en taxi?** *Kahn deu shih•ka ehn tax•ee*
Do you have the number for a taxi?	**Har du numret till taxi?** *Hahr deu nuhm•reht tihl tax•ee*
Pick me up at… (place/time)	**Hämta mig vid/klockan…** *hehm•ta may veed/kloh•kan…*
I'm going to…	**Jag ska resa till…** *yahg skah ree•sa tihl…*
this address	**denna adress** *deh•na ad•rehs*
the airport	**flygplatsen** *flewg•plat•sehn*
the train station	**järnvägsstationen** *yairn•vaigs•sta•shoa•nehn*
I'm late.	**Jag är sen.** *yahg air seen*
Can you drive faster/slower?	**Kan du köra fortare/långsammare?** *Kan deu chur•ra fohrt•a•rer/loang•sam•a•rer*
Stop/Wait here.	**Stanna/Vänta här.** *sta•na/vehn•ta hair*
How much?	**Hur mycket kostar det?** *heur mew•ker kos•tar dee*
You said it would cost…kronor.	**Du sa att det skulle kosta…kronor.** *deu sah at dee skuh•ler kos•ta…kroa•nohr*

Keep the change.   **Behåll växeln.**
                   be • hoal vehx • ehln

A receipt, please. **Kvittot, tack.**
                   kvih • tot tak

Taxis can be found at stands marked **Taxi.** You can also flag down a taxi in the street, especially near hotels and bus and train stations. Calling a taxi by phone is a third option; numbers are available from your concierge or a local phone book. The sign **Ledig** (free), when lit, indicates that the taxi is available.

YOU MAY HEAR...

Vart vill du åka?   Where to?
vart vihl deu oa • ka

Vilken adress?   What's the
vihl • kehn ad • rehs   address?

BICYCLE & MOTORBIKE

I'd like to hire...   **Jag skulle vilja hyra...**
                        yahg skuh • ler vihl • ya hew • ra...

a bicycle   **en cykel**
                        ehn sew • kehl

a moped   **en moped**
                        ehn moh • peed

a motorbike   **en motorcykel**
                        ehn moa • tohr • sew • kehl

How much per day/week?	**Hur mycket kostar det per dag/vecka?** *heur <u>mew</u> • ker <u>kos</u> • tar d**ee** pair dahg/ <u>veh</u> • ka*
Can I have a helmet/lock?	**Kan jag få en hjälm/ett cykelås?** *kan yahg f**oa** ehn yehlm/eht <u>sew</u> • kehl • l**oa**s*

YOU MAY HEAR...

Har du ett internationellt körkort? *hahr deu eht in • tehr • na • sh**oa** • <u>nehlt</u> <u>churr</u> • koart*	Do you have an international driver's license?
Kan jag få se ert pass, tack? *kan yahg f**oa** see eert pas tak*	May I see your passport, please?
Vill du ha en försäkring? *vil deu hah ehn furr • <u>sair</u> • krihng*	Do you want insurance?
Det blir en handpenning på... *d**ee** bleer ehn <u>hand</u> • peh • nihng p**oa**...*	There is a deposit of...
Underteckna här, tack. *<u>uhn</u> • der • tehk • <u>na</u> hair tak*	Please sign here.

CAR HIRE

Where can I hire a car?	**Var kan jag hyra en bil?** *vahr kan yahg <u>hew</u> • ra ehn beel*
I'd like to hire...	**Jag skulle vilja hyra...** *yahg <u>skuh</u> • ler <u>vihl</u> • ya <u>hew</u> • ra...*
a cheap/small car	**en billig/liten bil** *en bihl • eeg/lee • tehn beel*
a 2-/4-door car	**en bil med två/fyra dörrar** *ehn beel meed tv**oa**/<u>few</u> • ra <u>dur</u> • rar*

an automatic/ manual car	**en bil med automatväxel/ manuell** *ehn beel meed ah • toa • <u>maht</u> • vehx • ehl/ mah • nuh • ehl*
a car with air- conditioning	**en bil med luftkonditionering** *ehn beel meed <u>luhft</u> • kohn • dee • shoa • <u>neer</u> • ihng*
a car seat	**en bilbarnstol** *ehn beel • <u>barn</u> • stoal*
How much does it cost...?	**Hur mycket kostar det...?** *heur <u>mew</u> • ker <u>kos</u> • tar dee...*
per day/week	**per dag/vecka** *pair dahg/<u>veh</u> • ka*
per kilometer	**per kilometer** *pair chee • loh • <u>mee</u> • ter*
How much does it cost...?	**Hur mycket kostar det...?** *heur <u>mew</u> • ker <u>kos</u> • tar dee...*
for unlimited mileage	**för obegränsade mil** *furr oa • beh • <u>grehn</u> • sa • deh • meel*
with insurance	**med försäkring** *meed furr • <u>sair</u> • krihng*
Are there any special weekend rates?	**Har ni särskilda helgrabatter?** *hahr nee <u>sair</u> • shihl • da <u>hely</u> • ra • bat • ehr*

FUEL STATION

Where's the next fuel station, please?	**Ursäkta, var är närmaste bensinstation?** *<u>eur</u> • shehk • ta vahr air <u>nair</u> • mas • the behn • <u>seen</u> • sta • <u>shoan</u>*
Fill it up, please.	**Fyll tanken, tack.** *feyl <u>tan</u> • kehn tak*
...liters, please.	**...liter, tack...** *.<u>lee</u> • tehr tak*

I'll pay in cash/by credit card. | **Jag betalar kontant/med kreditkort.**
Yahg beh•tah•lar kohn•tant/meed kreh•deet•koart

YOU MAY SEE...	
VANLIG	regular
PREMIUM	premium [super]
DIESEL	diesel

ASKING DIRECTIONS

Is this the road to...?	**Är det här vägen till...?**
	air dee hair vair•gehn tihl...
How far is it to...?	**Hur långt är det till...?**
	heur loangt air dee tihl...
Where's...?	**Var ligger...?**
	vahr lih•gehr...
...Street	**...gata**
	...gah•ta
this address	**denna adress**
	deh•na ad•rehs
the highway [motorway]	**motorvägen**
	moa•tohr•vair•gehn
Can you show me on the map?	**Kan du visa mig på kartan?**
	kan deu vee•sa may poa kahr•tan
I'm lost.	**Jag har kommit vilse.**
	yahg hahr koh•miht vihl•ser

YOU MAY HEAR...

rakt fram	straight ahead
rahkt fram	
till vänster	on/to the left
tihl <u>vehn</u> • stehr	
till höger	on/to the right
tihl <u>hur</u> • gehr	
i/runt hörnan	on/around the corner
ee/ruhnt <u>hur</u> • nan	
mitt emot	opposite
miht ee • <u>moat</u>	
bakom	behind
<u>bah</u> • kohm	
bredvid	next to
<u>breh</u> • veed	
efter	after
<u>ehf</u> • tehr	
norr/söder	north/south
nohr/<u>sur</u> • dehr	
öster/väster	east/west
<u>urs</u> • tehr/<u>vehs</u> • tehr	
vid trafikljusen	at the traffic light
veed tra • <u>feek</u> • yeus • ehn	
vid avfarten	at the exit
veed <u>afv</u> • far • tehn	

YOU MAY SEE...

STOP	**STOPP**	stop
	LÄMNA FÖRETRÄDE	yield
	PARKERING FÖRBJUDEN	no parking
	FARLIG KURVA	dangerous curve
	ENKELRIKTAT	one way
	INGEN INFART	no entry
	OMKÖRNING FÖRBJUDEN	no passing
	U-SVÄNG FÖRBJUDEN	no U-turn
	ÖVERGÅNGSSTÄLLE FÖR FOTGÄNGARE	pedestrian crossing

PARKING

Can I park here?	**Får jag parkera här?**
	foar yahg par • kee • ra hair
Is there a parking lot [car park] nearby?	**Finns det en parkeringsplats i närheten?**
	fihns dee ehn par • kee • rihngs • plats ee nair • hee • tehn

Where's...?	**Var ligger...?**
	Vahr lih • gehr...
the parking garage	**parkeringshuset**
	par-kee • rihngs • huhseht
the parking meter	**parkeringsautomaten**
	par • kee • rihngs ah • toa • mah • tehn
How much does it cost...?	**Hur mycket koster det...?**
	heur mew • ker kos • tar dee...
per hour	**per timme**
	pair tihm • er
per day	**per dag**
	pair dahg
overnight	**över natten**
	ur • vehr na • tehn

Street parking, parking lots and, in some cases, parking garages will be available in most of Sweden's cities and larger towns. Street parking is generally metered in city centers and downtown areas. A blue circular sign with a red slash tells you where parking is prohibited. There will be signs indicating whether or not parking is free. In places where parking is metered, a ticket allowing you to park for a specific period of time will need to be purchased. If this is the case, tickets can be purchased from a **biljettautomat** (ticket machine). You pay for the amount of time you want to park and then place the ticket on the driver's side of the car, on the dashboard, so that the ticket is in plain sight. In some cases, parking may be free, and there will be signs posted with time limits, usually two or three hours.

BREAKDOWN & REPAIR

My car broke down/ won't start.	**Min bil har gått sönder/startar inte.** *min beel hahr goat <u>surn</u> • dehr/<u>star</u> • tar <u>in</u> • ter*
Can you fix it today?	**Kan ni laga den idag?** *kan nee <u>lah</u> • ga dehn ee • dahg*
When will it be ready?	**När blir den färdig?** *nair bleer dehn <u>fair</u> • dihg*
How much?	**Hur mycket kostar det?** *heur <u>mew</u> • ker <u>kos</u> • tar dee*
I have a puncture/ flat tyre (tire).	**Jag har punktering** *Yahg hahr puhng • teh • rihng*

ACCIDENTS

There's been an accident	**Det har hänt en olycka.** *dee hahr hehnt ehn <u>oa</u> • lew • ka*
Call an ambulance/ the police.	**Ring efter en ambulans/polisen.** *rihng <u>ehf</u> • ter ehn am • beu • <u>lans</u>/ poa • <u>lee</u> • sehn*

PLACES TO STAY

NEED TO KNOW

Can you recommend a hotel in...?	**Kan du rekommendera ett hotel i...?**
	kan deu reh • koh • mehn • dee • ra eht hoh • tehl ee...
I have a reservation.	**Jag har bokat rum.**
	yahg hahr boa • kat ruhm
My name is...	**Jag heter...**
	yahg hee • tehr...
Do you have a room...?	**Har ni ett ledigt rum...?**
	hahr nee eht lee • dihgt ruhm...
for one/two	**för en person/två personer**
	furr ehn pehr • shoan/tvoa pehr • shoan • ehr
with a bathroom	**med badrum**
	meed bahd • ruhm
with air-conditioning	**med luftkonditionering**
	meed luhft • kohn • dee • shoa • neer • ihng
For tonight.	**För ikväll.**
	furr ee • kvehl
For two nights.	**För två nätter.**
	furr tvoa neh • tehr
For one week.	**För en vecka.**
	furr ehn veh • ka
How much?	**Hur mycket kostar det?**
	heur mew • ker kos • tar dee

Do you have anything cheaper?	**Har ni någonting billigare?**
	hahr nee <u>noa</u> • gohn • tihng <u>bihl</u> • ee • ga • rer
When's check-out?	**När måste vi checka ut?**
	nair <u>mos</u> • ter vee <u>sheh</u> • ka eut
Can I leave this in the safe?	**Kan jag lämna detta i kassaskåpet?**
	Kan yahg <u>lehm</u> • na <u>deh</u> • ta ee <u>ka</u> • sah • <u>skoa</u> • peht
Could we leave our baggage here until...?	**Kan vi lämna vårt bagage här till klockan...?**
	kan vee <u>lehm</u> • na voart ba • <u>goash</u> hair tihl <u>kloh</u> • kan...
Could I have the bill/ receipt, please?	**Kan jag få räkningen/kvittot, tack?**
	Kan yahg foa <u>rairk</u> • nihng • en/ <u>kvih</u> • toht tak
I'll pay in cash/by credit card.	**Jag betalar kontant/med kreditkort.**
	Yahg beh • <u>tah</u> • lar kohn • <u>tant</u>/meed kreh • <u>deet</u> • koart

SOMEWHERE TO STAY

Can you recommend a hotel in...?	**Kan du rekommendera ett hotel i...?**
	kan deu reh • koh • mehn • dee • ra eht hoh • tehl ee...
a hostel	**ett vandrarhem**
	eht vand • rar • hehm
a campsite	**en kampingplats**
	ehn kam • pihng • plats
a bed and breakfast	**rum med frukost**
	ruhm mehd fruh • kohst
What is it near?	**Vad finns det i närheten?**
	vahd fihns dee ee nair • hee • tehn
How do I get there?	**Hur kommer jag dit?**
	heur • koh • mehr yahg deet

AT THE HOTEL

I have a reservation.	**Jag har bokat rum.**
	yahg hahr boh • kat ruhm
My name is...	**Jag heter...**
	yahg hee • tehr...
Do you have a room...?	**Har ni ett rum...?**
	hahr nee eht ruhm...
with a bathroom/ shower	**med bad/dusch**
	meed bahd/deush
with air-conditioning	**med luftkonditionering**
	meed luhft • kohn • dee • shoa • neer • ihng
that's smoking/	**för rökare/icke-rökare**
	furr rur • kah • rer/
non-smoking	*ih • keh rur • ka • rer*
For tonight.	**För ikväll.**
	furr ee • kvehl

YOU MAY HEAR...

Ert pass/kreditkort, tack.
ehrt pas/ kreh • deet • koart tak

Your passport/
credit card,
please.

Kan du fylla i den här blanketten.
*kan deu few • la ee dehn hair
blan • keh • tehn*

Skriv under här.
skreev uhn • der hair

Please fill out
this form.

Sign here.

For two nights.	**För två nätter.** *furr tvoa neh • tehr*
For one week.	**För en vecka.** *furr ehn veh • ka*
Does the hotel have...?	**Finns det...på hotellet?** *fihns dee...poa hoh • tehl • eht*
a computer	**en dator** *ehn dah • tohr*
an elevator [lift]	**en hiss** *ehn hihs*
(wireless) internet service	**(trådlös) internet** *(troad • lurs) in • tehr • net*
room service	**rumservice** *ruhm • sehr • vihs*
a pool	**en simbassäng** *ehn sihm • ba • sehng*
a gym	**ett gym** *eht ym*
I need...	**Jag behöver...** *yahg beh • hur • vehr...*
an extra bed	**en extra säng** *ehn ehx • tra sehng*

a cot	**en tältsäng**
	ehn <u>tehlt</u> • sehng
a crib	**en barnsäng**
	ehn <u>bahrn</u> • sehng

For Numbers, see page 22.

PRICE

How much per night/week?	**Vad kostar det per natt/vecka?**
	Vahd <u>kos</u> • tar dee pair nat/<u>veh</u> • ka
Does the price include breakfast/ sales tax [VAT]?	**Ingår frukost/moms i priset?**
	ihn • goar <u>fruh</u> • kohst/mohms ee <u>pree</u> • seht
Are there any discounts?	**Ger ni rabatter?**
	Yehr nee ra • bat·ehr

PREFERENCES

Can I see the room?	**Kan jag se rummet?**
	Kan yahg seh ruhm • eht
I'd like a…room.	**Jag skulle vilja ha ett…rum.**
	Yahg skuh • ler vihl • ya hah eht …ruhm
better	**bättre**
	beh • treh
bigger	**större**
	stuh • reh
cheaper	**billigare**
	bihl • ee • ga • rer
quieter	**tystare**
	tews • tah • rer
I'll take it.	**Ja tar det.**
	Yahg tahr deht
No, I won't take it.	**Nej, jag tar inte det.**
	Nay, yahg tahr deht in • ter

There is a wide range of places to stay in Sweden, from luxury to budget. Budget options include **privatrum** (private rooms), much like bed and breakfasts, or **stugor** (cabins) and **lägenheter** (apartments). Cabins and apartments are usually rented out on a weekly basis, but one- or two-night stays may also be an option. Information can be found at the local tourist office; you may also see signs along the road indicating that there is a vacancy in a cabin nearby. Motorists can look for **motel** (motels); these are reasonably priced with restaurants and car-friendly facilities. When looking for somewhere to stay in university towns such as Stockholm, Göteborg or Lund, staying at a **sommarhotel** (summer hotel) can be a good choice. Student dormitories are open to tourists in the summer and are a good option if you are traveling in a group. Families can enjoy a **familjehotell** (a family hotel), which has special rates for groups sharing the same room (three to six beds). These only operate during the summer months. All-inclusive accommodation is also available in the form of a **turisthotell** (tourist hotel) or **pensionat** (boarding house). These are clean and comfortable hotels or guesthouses that are often found at summer resorts and winter sport areas. Sweden also offers first class and deluxe hotels, usually found in larger cities and towns. Prices and amenities vary but the standards are usually high. Breakfast is usually included. When booking somewhere to stay during the summer months and high tourist season it is important to book in advance.

QUESTIONS

Where's...?	**Var ligger...?**
	vahr lih • gehr...
the bar	**baren**
	bah • rehn
the bathroom [toilet]	**toaletten**
	toa • ah • leh • tehn
the elevator [lift]	**hissen**
	his • ehn
Can I have...?	**Kan jag få...?**
	kan yahg foa...
a blanket	**ett täcke**
	eht teh • ker
an iron	**ett strykjärn**
	eht strewk • yairn
the room key/ key card	**rumsnyckeln/nyckelkortet**
	Ruhms • new • kehl/new • kehl • koart
a pillow	**en kudde**
	ehn keu • der
soap	**tvål**
	tvoal
toilet paper	**toalettpapper**
	toa • ah • leht • pa • pehr
a towel	**en handduk**
	ehn han • deuk
Can I use this adapter here?	**Kan jag använda den här adaptern här?**
	kan yahg an • vehn • da dehn hair a • dap • tern hair
How do I turn on the lights?	**Hur tänder man lamporna?**
	heur tehn • der man lam • pohr • na
Could you wake me at...?	**Kan ni väcka mig klockan...?**
	kan nee veh • ka may kloh • kan...

Could I have my things from the safe?

Kan jag få mina saker från kassaskåpet?
kan yahg foa mee • na sah • ker froan ka • sa • skoa • peht

Is there any mail/a message for me?

Finns det någon post/eht meddelande till mig?
fihns dee noa • gohn pohst/eht meed • deel • an • der tihl may

Do you have a laundry service?

Har ni tvättservice?
hahr nee tveht • sehr • vihs

YOU MAY SEE...

TRYCK	push
DRAG	pull
WC	restroom [toilet]
DAMTOALETT	women's restroom
HERRTOALETT	men's restroom
DUSCH	shower
HISS	elevator [lift]
TRAPPOR	stairs
TVÄTT	laundry
VAR GOD STÖR EJ	do not disturb
BRANDUTGÅNG	fire door
NÖDUTGÅNG	emergency exit
TELEFONVÄCKNING	wake-up call

PROBLEMS

There's a problem.	**Jag har ett problem.**
	yahg hahr eht proh • bleem
I've lost my key/ key card.	**Jag har tappat bort min nyckel/mitt nyckelkort.**
	yahg hahr ta • pat bort mihn new • kehl/ miht new • kehl • koart
I've locked myself out of my room.	**Jag har låst ut mig ur rummet.**
	yahg hahr loast eut may eur ruhm • eht
There's no hot water/ toilet paper.	**Det finns inget varmvatten/ toalettpapper.**
	dee fihns ihng • eht varmt • va • tehrn/ toa • ah • leht • pa • per
The room is dirty.	**Rummet är smutsigt.**
	ruhm • eht air smuht • siht
There are bugs in our room.	**Det finns insekter på vårt rum.**
	dee fihns ihn • sehk • tehr poa voart ruhm
Can you fix…?	**Kan ni laga…?**
	kan nee lah • ga…
the air- conditioning	**luftkonditioneringen**
	luhft • kohn • dee • shoa • neer • ihng • ehn
the fan	**fläkten**
	flehk • tehn
the heating	**värmen**
	vair • mehn
the light	**lampan**
	lahm • pan
the TV	**teven**
	teh • veen
the toilet	**toaletten**
	toa • ah • leh • tehn

I'd like to move to another room.
Jag skulle vilja flytta till ett annat rum.
yahg skuh • ler vihl • ya flew • ta tihl eht an • at ruhm

...is/are broken.
...är trasig.
...air trah • sihg

---

i

Throughout Sweden the current is 230-volt, 50-cycle AC. If you bring your own electrical appliances, buy a continental adapter plug (round pins) before leaving home. You may also need a transformer appropriate to the wattage of the appliance.

CHECKING OUT

When do we need to check out?
När måste vi checka ut?
nair mos • ter vee sheh • ka eut

Could we leave our baggage here until...?
Kan vi lämna vårt bagage här till klockan...?
kan vee lehm • na voart ba • goash hair tihl kloh • kan...

Can I have an itemized bill/receipt?
Kan jag få en specificerad räkning/ ett specificerad kvitto?
kan yahg foa ehn speh • seh • fee • ee • rad rairk • ning/eht speh • seh • fee • ee • rad kvih • toh

I think there's a mistake in this bill.
Jag tror det måste vara fel på notan.
Yahg troar dee mos • ter vah • ra feel poa noa • tan.

I'll pay in cash/by credit card.
Jag betalar kontant/med kreditkort.
Yahg beh • tah • lar kohn • tant/meed kreh • deet • koart

> ℹ️
>
> A service charge as well as **moms** (sales tax) is included in hotel and restaurant bills, but you are expected to round up a restaurant bill to the nearest **krona**. Tipping is generally not expected, but it's always appreciated if the service has been exceptionally good. It is customary to give a small tip to hairdressers, barbers, taxi drivers and porters.

RENTING

I've reserved an apartment/a room.	**Jag har bokat en lägenhet/ett rum.** *Yahg hahr <u>boh</u> • kat ehn <u>lair</u> • gehn • h<u>eet</u>/ eht ruhm*
My name is...	**Jag heter...** *yahg <u>hee</u> • tehr...*
Can I have the key/ key card?	**Kan jag få nyckeln/nyckelkortet?** *kan yahg foa <u>new</u> • kehln/ <u>new</u> • kehl • <u>koar</u> • teht*
Are there...?	**Finns det...?** *fihns d<u>ee</u>...*
dishes	**porslin** *poarsh • <u>leen</u>*
pillows	**kuddar** *<u>keu</u> • dar*
sheets	**lakan** *<u>lah</u> • kan*
towels	**handdukar** *han • d<u>eu</u> • kar*
utensils	**bestick** *beh • <u>stihk</u>*

When do I put out the bins/recycling?	**När ska jag ställa ut soporna/återvinning?**
	nair skah yahg <u>steh</u> • la eut <u>soa</u> • pohr • na/oat • ehr • vihn • ing
...has broken down.	**...har gått sönder.**
	...hahr goat <u>surn</u> • dehr
How does...work?	**Hur fungerar...?**
	heur fuhn • <u>geh</u> • rar...
the air-conditioner	**luftkonditioneringen**
	<u>luhft</u> • kohn • dee • shoa • <u>neer</u> • ihng • ehn
the dishwasher	**diskmaskinen**
	dihsk • ma • <u>shee</u> • nehn
the freezer	**frysen**
	<u>frew</u> • sen
the heater	**värmeelementet**
	<u>vair</u> • meh • ehl • eh • <u>mehn</u> • teht
the microwave	**mikrovågsugnen**
	mik • roh • v<u>oa</u>gs • <u>eung</u> • nehn
How does...work?	**Hur fungerar...?**
	heur fuhn • <u>geh</u> • rar...
the refrigerator	**kylskåpet**
	kewl • <u>skoa</u> • peht
the stove	**spisen**
	<u>spee</u> • sehn
the washing machine	**tvättmaskinen**
	tveht • mah • <u>shee</u> • nehn

DOMESTIC ITEMS

I'd like...	**Jag skulle vilja ha...**
	yahg <u>skuh</u> • ler <u>vihl</u> • ya hah...
an adapter	**en adapter**
	ehn a • <u>dap</u> • tehr
aluminum	**aluminiumfolie**
	ah • leu • <u>mee</u> • nee • um • foh • lyer foil

a bottle opener	**en flasköppnare**
	ehn flask • urp • na • rer
a broom	**en sopborste**
	ehn sop • borsh • ter
a can opener	**en konservöppnare**
	ehn kohn • serv • urp • na • rer
cleaning supplies	**städutrustning**
	staird • eut • reust • nihng
a corkscrew	**en korkskruv**
	ehn kohrk • skreuv
detergent	**tvättmedel**
	tveht • mee • dehl
dishwashing liquid	**diskmedel**
	disk • mee • dehl
bin bags	**soppåsar**
	sop • poa • sar
a light bulb	**en glödlampa**
	ehn glurd • lam • pa
matches	**tändstickor**
	tehnd • stih • kohr
a mop	**en skurmopp**
	ehn skewr • mop
napkins	**pappersservetter**
	pa • pers • sahr • veh • ter
plastic wrap	**plastfolie**
[cling film]	*plast • foh • lyer*
a plunger	**en vaskrensare**
	ehn vask • rehn • sa • rer
scissors	**en sax**
	ehn sax
a vacuum cleaner	**en dammsugare**
	ehn damm • seu • ga • rer

For In the Kitchen, see page 199.

(i)

If you are looking for something comfortable and reasonably priced, **Svenska Turistföreningen** or **STF** (the Swedish Tourist Club) is an excellent place to start. Here you can search for accommodations such as **vandrarhem** (youth hostels). If you are a member of **STF** or Hostelling International you get a member discount. Generally, room options include dormitory style rooms, split male and female, as well as smaller private rooms or family rooms. You are usually expected to bring your own towels and sheets as these usually are not provided, but can be rented. Shared kitchen facilities are often available, so that you can buy food at the local supermarket and prepare your own meals. Some hostels offer breakfast.

AT THE HOSTEL

Do you have any places left for tonight?	**Finns det några lediga platser ikväll?** *fihns d**ee** n**oa** • gra l**ee** • dih • ga plats • ehr ee • kvehl*
Can I have…?	**Kan jag få…?** *kan yahg foa…*
a single/double room	**ett enkelrum/dubbelrum** *eht hng • kehl • ruhm/duh • behl • ruhm*
a blanket	**ett täcke** *eht tehk • er*
a pillow	**en kudde** *ehn keu • der*
sheets	**lakan** *lah • kan*
a towel	**en handduk** *ehn han • deuk*

What time are the doors locked?	**När stängs ytterdörrarna?**
	nair stehngs **ew**•ter•dur•ar•na
Do I need a membership card?	**Behöver jag medlemskort?**
	beh•hur•vehr yahg mehd•lehms•koart
Here's my international student card.	**Här är mitt internationella studentkort.**
	hair air miht in•tehr•na•shoa•nehl•ah stuh•dehnt•koart

GOING CAMPING

Can I camp here?	**Får man tälta här?**
	**foar** man **tehl**•ta hair
Is there a campsite near here?	**Finns det en campingplats i närheten?**
	fihns dee ehn **kam**•pihng•plats ee **nair**•hee•tehn
What is the charge per day/week?	**Vad kostar det per dag/vecka?**
	vahd **kos**•tar dee pair dahg/**veh**•ka
Are there...?	**Finns det...?**
	fihns dee...
cooking facilities	**kokmöjligheter**
	**koak**•mury•lihg•hee•tehr
electrical outlets	**nätuttag**
	**nairt**•eut•tahg
laundry facilities	**tvättmöjligheter**
	**tveht**•mury•lig•hee•tehr
showers	**dusch**
	deush
tents for hire	**tält för uthyrning**
	tehlt furr **eut**•hewr•nihng
Where can I empty the chemical toilet?	**Var kan jag tömma den kemiska toaletten?**
	vahr kan yahg **tur**•ma dehn **sheh**•mihs•ka toa•ah•**leh**•tehn

For Domestic Items, see page 80.

YOU MAY SEE...

DRICKSVATTEN	drinking water
INGEN CAMPING	no camping
INGEN GRILLNING	no barbeques
INGEN ÖPPEN ELD	no fires

COMMUNICATIONS

NEED TO KNOW

Where's an internet cafe?	**Var finns det ett internetkafé?** *vahr fihns dee eht ihn • tehr • neht • ka • feh*
Can I access the internet/check e-mail here?	**Kan jag komma ut på internet/ kola e-post här?** *kan yahg koh • ma eut poa ihn • tehr • neht/koa • la ee • pohst hair*
How much per hour/ half hour?	**Hur mycket kostar det per timme/ halvtimme?** *heur mew • ker kos • tar dee pair tihm • er/halv • tihm • er*
How do I connect/ log on?	**Hur loggar jag in?** *heur loh • gar yag ihn*
Can I have a phone card?	**Kan jag få ett telefonkort?** *kan yahg foa eht teh • leh • foan • koart*

Can I have your phone number?	**Kan jag få ditt telefonnummer?** *kan yahg foa diht teh•leh•foan•nuhm•ehr*
Here's my number/ e-mail address.	**Här är mitt nummer/min e-postadress.** *hair air miht nuhm•ehr/mihn ee•pohst•ad•rehs*
Call me.	**Var snäll och ring mig.** *vahr snehl ohk ring may*
E-mail me.	**Skicka en e-post till mig.** *shih•ka ehn ee•pohst tihl may*
Hello. This is...	**Hej. Det här är...** *hay dee hair air...*
I'd like to speak to...	**Jag skulle vilja tala med...** *yahg skuh•ler vihl•ya tah•la meed...*
Repeat that, please.	**Kan du upprepa det, tack.** *kan deu uhp•ree•pa dee tak*
I'll be in touch.	**Jag hör av mig snart.** *yahg hur afv may snahrt*
Goodbye.	**Hej då.** *hay doa*
Where is the post office?	**Var ligger posten?** *vahr lih•gehr pohs•tehn*
I'd like to send this to...	**Jag skulle vilja skicka det här till...** *yahg skuh•ler vihl•ya shih•ka dee hair tihl...*

ONLINE

Where's an internet cafe?	**Var finns det ett internetcafe?**
	vahr fihns deht eht
	ihn • tehr • neht • ka • feh
Does it have wireless internet?	**Finns det trådlös internet där?**
	fihns dee troad • lurs ihn • tehr • neht dair
What is the WiFi password?	**Vilket är WiFi-lösenordet?**
	vihl • keht wai • fai-lur • sehn • oarde
Is the WiFi free?	**Är WiFi:n gratis?**
	air wai • fain grah • tihs
Do you have bluetooth?	**Har ni blåtand?**
	hahr nee bloa • tand
How do I turn the computer on/off?	**Hur sätter jag på/stänger jag av datorn?**
	heur seh • tehr yahg poa/stehng • her yahg afv dah • torn
Can I print?	**Kan jag skriva ut?**
	kan yahg skree • va eut
Can I...?	**Kan jag...?**
	kahn yahg...
access the internet	**gå ut på internet**
	goa eut poa ihn • tehr • neth

check my e-mail	**kolla min e-post**
	kohla meen eh • pohst
plug in/charge my laptop/iPhone/ iPad/BlackBerry?	**sätta i/ladda min laptop/iPhone/ iPad/BlackBerry**
	sehta ih/ladha meen laptop/iPad/ BlackBerry
access Skype?	**använda Skype**
	an • vehn • a Skype
How much per half hour/hour?	**Hur mycket kostar det per halvtimme/ timme?**
	Heur mew • keh koh • star deht pehr halv • tihm • er/tih • mer
How do I...?	**Hur gör man för att...?**
	heur yurr man furr at...
connect/ disconnect	**koppla upp/koppla ner**
	kohp • la uhp/kohp • la nehr
log on/off	**logga in/ut**
	loh • ga ihn/eut
type this symbol	**skriva in det här tecknet**
	skree • va ihn dee hair tehk • neht
What's your e-mail?	**Vad har du för e-postadress?**
	vahd hahr deu furr ee • pohst • ad • rehs
My e-mail is...	**Min e-postadress är...**
	mihn ee • pohst • ad • rehs air...
Do you have a scanner?	**Har ni en skanner?**
	Hahr nee ehn ska • nehr

SOCIAL MEDIA

Are you on Facebook/Twitter?	**Finns du på Facebook/Twitter?**
	Fihns deu poa Facebook/Twitter
What's your user name?	**Vilket användarnamn har du?**
	Vihl • keht an • vehn • dar • namn hahr deu
I'll add you as a friend.	**Jag lägger till dig som vän.**
	yahg lehg • ehr tihl day sohm vehn

I'll follow you on Twitter.	**Jag följer dig på Twitter.**
	Yahg fuhl•yehr day poa Twitter
Are you following…?	**Följer du…?**
	Fuhl•yehr deu…
I'll put the pictures on Facebook/Twitter.	**Jag lägger ut bilderna på Facebook/Twitter.**
	yahg lehg•ehr eut bihl•dehr•na poa Facebook/Twitter
I'll tag you in the pictures.	**Jag taggar bilderna.**
	yahg ta•gar bihl•dehr•na

YOU MAY SEE…

STÄNG	close
RADERA	delete
E-POST	e-mail
UTGÅNG	exit
HJÄLP	help
INSTANT MESSENGER	instant messenger
INTERNET	internet
LOGGA IN	login
NYTT MEDDELANDE	new message
AV/PÅ	on/off
ÖPPNA	open
SKRIV UT	print
SPARA	save
SKICKA	send
ANVÄNDARNAMN	username
LÖSENORD	password
TRÅDLÖS INTERNET	wireless internet

PHONE

A phone card/ prepaid phone please.	**Ett telefonkort, tack.** *eht teh • leh • foan • koart tak*
How much does it cost?	**Hur mycket kostar det?** *heur mew • ker kos • tar dee*
What's the area/ country code for…?	**Vad är riktnumret/landskoden till…?** *vahd air rikt • nuhm • reht/ lands • koa • dehn tihl…*
What's the number for Information?	**Vilket nummer är det till Nummerbyrån?** *vihl • keht nuhm • ehr air dee tihl nuhm • ehr • bew • roan*
I'd like the number for…	**Jag skulle vilja ha numret till…** *yahg skuh • ler vihl • ya hah nuhm • reht tihl…*
I'd like to call collect [reverse the charges].	**Jag vill ringa ett mottagaren-betalar-samtal.** *yahg vihl rihng • a eht moh • tah • ga • ren be • tah • lar-sam • tahl*
My phone doesn't work here.	**Min telefon fungerar inte här.** *mihn teh • leh • foan fuhn • geh • rar ihn • ter hair*
What network are you on?	**Vilket nätverk använder du?** *vihl • keht neht • vehrk an • vehn • der deu*
Is it 3G?	**Är det 3G?** *air deht treh • geh*
I have run out of credit/minutes.	**Jag har inte mer pengar/minuter på kortet.** *yahg hahr ihn • ther meer pehng • ar/ mih • nuh • tehr poa koart • eht*
Can I buy some credit?	**Kan jag fylla på kortet?** *kahn yahg fewlah poa koart • et*

Do you have a phone charger?	**Har du/ni en telefonladdare?** *Hahr deu/nee ehn teh • leh • foan • lad • ar • eh*
Can I have your number?	**Kan jag få ditt telefonnummer?** *kan yahg foa diht teh • leh • <u>foan</u> • nuhm • ehr*
Here's my number.	**Här är mitt nummer.** *hair air miht <u>nuhm</u> • ehr*
Please call me.	**Var snäll och ring mig.** *vahr snehl ohk rihng may*
Please text me.	**Var snäll och skicka ett sms till mig.** *Vahr snehl ohk <u>shih</u> • ka eht ehs • ehm • ehs tihl may*
I'll call you.	**Jag ringer dig.** *yahg <u>rihng</u> • ehr day*
I'll text you.	**Jag skickar ett sms till dig.** *yahg <u>shih</u> • kar eht ehs • ehm • ehs tihl day*

TELEPHONE ETIQUETTE

Hello. This is…	**Hej. Det här är…** *hay dee hair air…*
I'd like to speak to…	**Jag skulle vilja tala med…** *yahg <u>skuh</u> • ler <u>vihl</u> • ya <u>tah</u> • la meed…*
Extension…	**Anknytning…** *<u>an</u> • knewt • nihng…*
Speak louder/more slowly.	**Var snäll och tala högre/långsammare.** *vahr snehl ohk <u>tah</u> • la <u>hur</u> • greh/ <u>loang</u> • sam • a • rer*
Can you repeat that?	**Kan du upprepa det?** *kan deu <u>uhp</u> • ree • pa dee*
I'll call back later.	**Jag ringer senare.** *yahg <u>rihng</u> • ehr <u>see</u> • na • rer*
Goodbye.	**Hej då.** *hay doa*

YOU MAY HEAR...

Vem är det?	Who's calling?
vehm air dee	
Ett ögonblick.	One moment.
eht <u>ur</u> • gohn • blihk	
Tyvärr, är han/hon inte här.	I'm afraid he/
<u>tew</u> • vair air hahn/hoan <u>ihn</u> • ter hair	she is not in.
Han/Hon kan inte komma till telefonen.	He/She can't
hahn/hoan kan <u>ihn</u> • ter <u>koh</u> • ma tihl	come to the
teh • leh • <u>foan</u> • ehn	phone.
Vill du lämna ett meddelande?	Would you like
vihl deu <u>lehm</u> • na eht <u>mee</u> • dee • lan • der	to leave a
	message?
Ring tillbaka senare/om tio minuter.	Call back later/
rihng tihl • <u>bah</u> • ka <u>see</u> • na • rer/	in 10 minutes.
ohm <u>tee</u> • oah mih • <u>neu</u> • tehr	
Kan han/hon ringa upp dig?	Can he/she
kan hahn/ hoan <u>rihng</u> • a uhp day	call you back?
Vad är ditt telefonnummer?	What's your
vahd air dihtteh • leh • <u>foan</u> • nuhm • her	number?

FAX

Can I send/receive a fax here?	**Kan man skicka/ta emot fax här?**
	kan man <u>shih</u> • ka/ta ee • <u>moat</u> fax hair
What's the fax number?	**Vad är ditt faxnummer?**
	vahd air diht fax • <u>nuhm</u> • ehr
Please fax this to…	**Var snäll och faxa det här till…**
	vahr snehl ohk <u>fax</u> • ah dee hair tihl…

ⓘ

To call the U.S. or Canada from Sweden, dial 00 + 1 + area code + phone number. To call the U.K., dial 00 + 44 + area code (minus first 0) + phone number. Information on area codes for Sweden and international dialing codes can be found in the phone book and are usually available at hotels and youth hostels. The emergency number in Sweden is 112.

POST

Where's the post office/mailbox?	**Var ligger posten/postlådan?** vahr <u>lih</u> • gehr pohs • tehn/ <u>pohst</u> • loa • dan
A stamp for this postcard/letter, please.	**Kan jag få ett frimärke till det här vykortet/brevet, tack.** kan yahg **foa** eht <u>free</u> • mair • ker tihl dee hair <u>vew</u> • koar • teht/ <u>bree</u> • veht tak
How much does it cost?	**Hur mycket kostar det?** heur <u>mew</u> • ker kos • tar dee
I want to send this package by airmail/express.	**Jag vill skicka det här paketet med flygpost/express.** yahg vihl <u>shih</u> • ka dee hair pa • <u>kee</u> • teht meed <u>flewg</u> • pohst/<u>ehx</u> • prehs
The receipt, please.	**Kvittot, tack.** <u>kvih</u> • toht tak

YOU MAY HEAR...

Fyll i tulldeklarationen, tack.
fewl ee tuhl • deh • klar • a • shoa • nehn tak

Please fill out the customs declaration form.

Vad är värdet?
vahd air vair • deht

What's the value?

Vad finns inuti?
vahd fihns ihn • eu • tee

What's inside?

Posten (the post office) is easy to find, just look for the blue **Post** sign with a yellow horn. Mailboxes are bright yellow. Business hours are 9:00 a.m. to 6:00 p.m. and until 1:00 p.m. on Saturdays. Like many other stores and business, you will need to take a number and wait for it to be called or displayed on a screen before you can be helped. Stamps can be purchased at **Pressbyrån** (newsstand chain) as well as some grocery stores.

SIGHTSEEING

NEED TO KNOW

Where's the tourist information office?	**Var ligger turistinformationen?** *vahr <u>lih</u> • gehr teu • <u>rihst</u> • ihn • fohr • ma • <u>shoan</u> • ehn*
What are the main points of interest?	**Vad finns det för sevärdheter?** *vahd fihns dee furr <u>see</u> • vaird • hee • tehr*
Do you have tours in English?	**Finns det några turer på engelska?** *fihns dee <u>noa</u> • gra teu • rehr poa ehng • ehl • ska*
Can I have a map/ guide, please?	**Kan jag få en karta/guide, tack?** *kan yahg foa ehn <u>kahr</u> • ta/gujd tak*

TOURIST INFORMATION

Do you have any information on...?	**Har ni information om...?** *hahr nee ihn • for • ma • <u>shoan</u> om...*
Can you recommend...?	**Kan ni rekommendera...?** *kan nee reh • koh • mehn <u>dee</u> • ra...*

(i)

There are tourist information offices in all large cities and towns. These are usually marked by a green sign with an **I**. For general information, Sweden's official tourism website is a good place to start. Here you can find information on accommodation, attractions and activities as well as cultural and historical information. Most cities have their own tourist boards and websites, where you can request brochures, maps and more prior to your arrival. Also look for **Stockholmskortet** (the Stockholm Card) if you will be spending several days in the city. For one fee, you have access to musems, events and transportation throughout the city. You can choose whether you want the card for 24, 48 or 72 hours. The equivalent in Göteborg is **Göteborgs Passet**.

a boat trip	**en båttur**
	ehn <u>boat</u> • teur
an excursion	**en rundtur**
	ehn <u>ruhnd</u> • teur
a sightseeing tour	**en sightseeingtur**
	ehn <u>sight</u> • see • ihng • teur

ON TOUR

I'd like to go on the tour to...	**Jag vill följa med på turen till...**
	yahg vihl <u>furl</u> • ja meed poa <u>teu</u> • ren tihl...
When's the next tour?	**När går nästa rundresa?**
	nair goar nehsta ruhnd • rehsa
Are there tours in English?	**Finns det någon tur på engelska?**
	fihns dee <u>noa</u> • gohn teur poa <u>ehng</u> • ehl • ska

Is there an English-speaking guide/audio guide?	**Finns det en engelsktalande guide/ljudguide?**
	fihns deht ehn ehng • ehlsk • tah • lan • de gahyd/ aw • dee • oh gahyd
What time do we leave/return?	**När åker vi/kommer vi tillbaka?**
	nair <u>oak</u> • er vee/<u>koh</u> • mehr vee tihl • <u>bah</u> • ka
We'd like to have a look at...	**Vi skulle vilja se...**
	vee <u>skuh</u> • ler vihl • ya see...
Can we stop here...?	**Kan vi stanna här...?**
	kan vee <u>sta</u> • na hair...
to take photographs	**för att ta foton**
	furr at tah <u>foa</u> • tohn
to buy souvenirs	**för att köpa souvenirer**
	furr at <u>chur</u> • pa seu • veh • <u>nee</u> • rehr
to use the toilets	**för att gå på toaletten**
	furr at goa poa toa • ah • <u>leh</u> • tehn
Is there access for the disabled?	**Finns det tillgång för rörelsehindrade?**
	fihns dee tihl • <u>goa</u>ng furr <u>rurr</u> • ehl • ser • <u>hihn</u> • dra • der

For Tickets, see page 45.

SEEING THE SIGHTS

Where is...?	**Var ligger...?**
	vahr <u>lih</u> • gehr...
the battleground	**slagfältet**
	<u>slahg</u> • fehl • teht
the botanical garden	**botaniska trädgården**
	boa • <u>tan</u> • ihs • ska traird • goar • dehn
Where is...?	**Var ligger...?**
	vahr <u>lih</u> • gehr...
the castle	**slottet**
	<u>sloht</u> • eht

the downtown area	**centrum**
	sehn • truhm
the fountain	**fontänen**
	fohn • _tairn_ • ehn
the library	**biblioteket**
	bihb • lee • oa • _teek_ • eht
the market	**torget**
	tohr • yeht
the museum	**museet**
	muh • _see_ • eht
the old town	**gamla stan**
	gam • la stahn
the opera house	**operan**
	oap • eh • ran
the palace	**slottet**
	sloht • eht
the park	**parken**
	park • ehn
the shopping area	**Et affärscentrumet**
	eht a • _ffairs_ • sehn • truhm • eht
the town hall	**stadshuset**
	stads • heus • eht
Can you show me on the map?	**Kan du visa mig på kartan?**
	kan deu vee • sa may poa _kahr_ • tan

It's...	**Det är...**
	det air...
amazing	**fantastiskt**
	fan • ta • stihskt
beautiful	**vackert**
	<u>*va*</u> • *kehrt*
boring	**trist**
	trihst
interesting	**intressant**
	in • treh • <u>sant</u>
magnificent	**storslaget**
	<u>*stoar*</u> • *slahg • eht*
romantic	**romantiskt**
	roh • <u>man</u> • tihskt
strange	**konstigt**
	kohn • stihgt
stunning	**förbluffande**
	furr·bluh·fahnder
terrible	**hemskt**
	hehmskt
ugly	**fult**
	feult
I (don't) like it.	**Jag tycker (inte) om den/det.**
	yahg <u>tew</u> • kehr (<u>in</u> • ter) ohm dehn/dee

For Asking Directions, see page 64.

RELIGIOUS SITES

Where is...?	**Var är...?**
	vahr air...
the cathedral	**domkyrkan**
	dohm • chewr • kahn
the church	**kyrkan**
	<u>*chewr*</u> • *kan*

the mosque	**moskén**
	mos • kehn
the shrine	**altaret**
	alt • a • reht
the synagogue	**synagogan**
	sihn • a • gohg • an
the temple	**templet**
	tehmp • leht
What time is mass/ the service?	**Hur dags är mässan/gudstjänsten?**
	heur daks air mehs • an/ geuds • tjain • stehn

ACTIVITIES

SHOPPING

NEED TO KNOW

Where is the market/mall [shopping centre]?	**Var ligger orget/affärscentrumet?** *vahr lih • gehr tohr • yeht/ a • ffairs • sehn • truhm • eht*
I'm just looking.	**Jag tittar bara.** *yahg tih • tar bah • ra*
Can you help me?	**Kan du hjälpa mig?** *kan deu yehlp • a may*
I'm being helped.	**Jag får hjälp, tack.** *yahg foar yehlp tak*
How much does it cost?	**Hur mycket kostar det?** *heur mew • ker kos • tar det*
This/That one, thanks.	**Den här/där, tack.** *dehn hair/dair tak*
That's all, thanks.	**Det var allt, tack.** *dee vahr alt tak*
Where do I pay?	**Var kan jag betala?** *vahr kan yahg beh • tah • la*
I'll pay in cash/by credit card.	**Jag vill betala kontant/med kreditkort.** *yahg vihl beh • tah • la kohn • tant/ meed kreh • deet • koart*
A receipt, please.	**Kvittot, tack.** *kvih • tot tak*

AT THE SHOPS

Where is...?	**Var finns...?** *vahr fihns...*

the antiques store	**antikaffären**
	an • teek • a • ffair • ehn
the bakery	**bageriet**
	bahg • eh • ree • eht
the bookstore	**bokhandeln**
	boak • han • dehln
the clothing store	**klädaffären**
	klaird • a • ffair • ehn
the delicatessen	**delikatessaffären**
	dehl • eh • ka • tehs • a • fair • ehn
the department store	**varuhuset**
	vahr • eu • heus • eht
the health food store	**hälsokostaffären**
	hehl • soa • kost • a • fair • ehn
the jeweler	**juveleraren**
	yeu • veh • lee • rar • ehn
the liquor store [off-licence]	**systembolaget**
	sews • teem • boa • lahg • eht
the market	**torget**
	tohr • yeht
the pastry shop	**konditoriet**
	kohn • deh • toh • ree • eht
the pharmacy [chemist]	**apoteket**
	a • poa • tee • keht
the produce [grocery] store	**livsmedelsaffären**
	lihvs • mee • dehls • a • fair • ehn
the shoe store	**skoaffären**
	skoa • a • fair • ehn
the shopping mall [shopping centre]	**affärscentrumet**
	a • ffairs • sehn • truhm • eht
the souvenir store	**souvenirbutiken**
	seu • veh • neer • buh • tee • kehn
the supermarket	**snabbköpet**
	snab • chur • peht

(i)

Although Sweden still has many small, specialty shops, **Köpcentrum** (malls) are becoming more and more common, especially in larger towns. Many chain and department stores, such as **Åhléns** and **Kappahl** and **Hennes & Mauritz**, have branches all over the country, all of which sell quality goods. In the well-established Stockholm department store **NK**, you can find almost anything, though it can be quite expensive. Designer goods can be found at **DesignTorget** in Stockholm. For traditional handicrafts look for signs with **hemslöjd** (handicraft); in Stockholm, these can be found at **Svensk Hemslöjd** and **Svenskt Hantverk** (traditional handicraft stores). Many towns have colorful markets, where you can buy anything from fresh fruit and vegetables to flowers and handicrafts. **Julmarknaden** (Christmas market) in Stockholm in the Old Town and **Skansen** (outdoor park and museum), are historic shopping areas.

Where is…?	**Var finns…?**
	vahr fihns…
the tobacconist	**tobaksaffären**
	toa • baks • a • ffair • ehn
the toy store	**leksaksaffären**
	leek • sahks • a • fair • ehn

ASK AN ASSISTANT

When do you open/ close?	**När öppnar/stänger ni?**
	nair uhp • nar/stehng • er nee
Where is…?	**Var finns…?**
	vahr fihns…

the cashier [cash desk]	**kassan**
	kah • san
the escalator	**rulltrappan**
	ruhl • tra • pan
the elevator [lift]	**hissen**
	his • ehn
the fitting room	**provrummet**
	proav • ruhm • eht
the store directory [guide]	**informationen**
	in • for • ma • _shoa_ • nehn
Can you help me?	**Kan du hjälpa mig?**
	kan deu _yehl_ • pa may
I'm just looking.	**Jag tittar bara.**
	yahg _tih_ • tar _bah_ • ra
I'm being helped.	**Tack, jag får hjälp.**
	tak yahg foar yehlp
Do you have any...?	**Har ni några...?**
	hahr nee _noa_ • gra...
Could you show	**Kan du visa mig några...?**
	kan deu _vee_ • sa
me...?	may _noa_ • gra...
Can you ship/ wrap it?	**Kan du skicka/slå in det?**
	kan deu _shih_ • ka dee/_sloa_ ihn dee
How much does it cost?	**Hur mycket kostar det?**
	heur _mew_ • kerht _kos_ • tar dee
That's all, thanks.	**Det var allt, tack.**
	dee vahr alt tak

For Clothes & Accessories, see page 114.

YOU MAY HEAR...

Kan jag hjälpa er?
kan yahg yehl • pa her

Can I help you?

Ett ögonblick, tack.
eht ur • gohn • blihk tak

Just a moment, please.

Vad vill ni beställa?
vahd vihl nee beh • steh • la

What would you like?

Något annat?
noa • goht an • nat

Anything else?

PERSONAL PREFERENCES

I want something...	**Jag skulle vilja ha något...** *yahg skuh • ler vihl • ya hah noa • goht...*
cheap/expensive	**billigt/dyrt** *bihl • igt/dewyt*
larger/smaller	**större/mindre** *sturr • er/mihn • drer*
from this region	**från denna region** *frohn deh • na regheoan*
Is it real?	**Är den äkta?** *air dehn aik • ta*
Could you show me this/that?	**Kan du visa mig den här/där?** *kan deu vee • sa may dehn hair/dair*
That's not quite what I want.	**Det är inte riktigt vad jag vill ha.** *dee air ihn • ter rihk • tikt vahd yahg vihl hah*
I don't like it.	**Jag tycker inte om det.** *yahg tew • kehr ihn • ter ohm dee*
That's too expensive.	**Det är för dyrt.** *dee air furr dewrt*

I'd like to think about it.	**Jag behöver tänka på det.** *Yahg beh • <u>hur</u> • vehr <u>tehng</u> • ka poa dee*
I'll take it.	**Jag tar den.** *yahg tahr dehn*

YOU MAY SEE...

ÖPPET/STÄNGT	open/closed
STÄNGT FÖR LUNCH	closed for lunch
PROVRUM	fitting room
KASSÖR/KASSÖRSKA	cashier
ENDAST KONTANT	cash only
VI TAR KREDITKORT	credit cards accepted
AFFÄRSTID	business hours
UTGÅNG	exit

PAYING & BARGAINING

How much does it cost?	**Hur mycket kostar det?** *heur <u>mew</u> • ker <u>kos</u> • tar dee*
I'll pay...	**Jag betalar...** *yahg beh • <u>tah</u> • lar...*
in cash	**kontant** *kohn • <u>tant</u>*
by credit card	**med kreditkort** *meed kreh • <u>deet</u> • koart*
by traveler's check [cheque]	**med en resecheck** *meed ehn <u>ree</u> • seh • shehk*
The receipt, please.	**Kvittot, tack.** *<u>kvih</u> • toht tak*

That's too much.	**Det är för mycket.**	
	dee air furr <u>mew</u> • ker	
I'll give you…	**Jag kan ge er…**	
	yahg kan yee ehr…	
I only have…kronor.	**Jag har bara…kronor.**	
	yahg hahr <u>bah</u> • ra…<u>kroa</u> • nohr	
Is that your best price?	**Är det ditt bästa pris?**	
	air deht diht beh • sta prihs	
Can you give me a discount?	**Kan du ge mig rabatt?**	
	kan deu yee may ra • <u>bat</u>	

For Numbers, see page 22.

YOU MAY HEAR…

Hur vill ni betala?
heur vihl nee beh • <u>tah</u> • la
How are you paying?

Ditt kreditkort har avvisats.
diht kreh • dith • koart hahr ahv • veesahts
Your credit card has been declined.

ID, tack.
ee • deh, tak.
ID, please.

Vi tar inte kreditkort.
Vee tahr ihnte kreh • diht • koart
We don't accept credit cards.

Bara kontanter, tack.
<u>bah</u> • ra kohn • <u>tan</u> • tehr tak
Cash only, please.

Har du mindre växel?
hahr deu <u>mihn</u> • drer <u>vehx</u> • ehl
Do you have any smaller change?

MAKING A COMPLAINT

I'd like...	**Jag skulle vilja...**
	yahg <u>skuh</u> • ler vihl • ya...
to exchange this	**byta den här**
	<u>bew</u> • ta dehn hair
to return this	**återlämna den här**
	<u>oa</u> • tehr • lehm • na dehn hair
a refund	**ha pengarna tillbaka**
	hah <u>pehng</u> • ar • na tihl • <u>bah</u> • ka
to see the manager	**få träffa butikschefen**
	foa <u>treh</u> • fa beu • <u>teeks</u> • sheef • ehn

SERVICES

Can you recommend...?	**Kan du rekommendera...?**
	kan deu reh • koh • mehn • <u>dee</u> • ra...
a barber	**en herrfrisör**
	ehn <u>hair</u> • fri • <u>surr</u>
a dry cleaner	**en kemtvätt**
	ehn <u>shehm</u> • tveht
a hairdresser	**en damfrisör**
	ehn <u>dahm</u> • free • <u>surr</u>
a laundromat [launderette]	**en snabbtvätt**
	ehn <u>snab</u> • tveht
a nail salon	**en nagelvårdssalong**
	ehn <u>nah</u> • gehl • <u>voards</u> • sa • <u>loang</u>
a spa	**ett spa**
	eht spah
a travel agency	**en resebyrå**
	ehn <u>ree</u> • seh • bew • roa
Can you...this?	**Kan ni...den här?**
	kan nee...dehn hair

alter	**ändra på**
	ehn • dra p**oa**
clean	**göra ren**
	y**ur** • ra reen
mend	**laga**
	lah • ga
press	**stryka**
	strew • ka
When will it be ready?	**När blir det klart?**
	nair bleer d**ee** klahrt

HAIR & BEAUTY

I'd like…	**Jag vill…**
	yahg vihl…
an appointment for today/ tomorrow	**boka en tid till idag/imorgon**
	boa • ka ehn teed tihl ee • dahg/ ee • _mo_ • ron
some colour/ highlights	**färg/slingor**
	fehry/slihng • ohr
my hair styled/ blow-dried	**få en ny frisyr/föning**
	foa ehn new free • _sewr_/funeeng
a hair cut	**få en klippning**
	foa ehn _klihp_ • nihng
an eyebrow/ a bikini wax	**en vaxning av ögonbrynen/bikinilinjen**
	ehn _vaks_ • nihng afv _ur_ • gonn • br**ew** • nehn/ beh • _kee_ • nee • _leen_ • yehn
a facial	**en ansiktsbehandling**
	ehn _an_ • sihkts • beh _hand_ • lihng
a manicure/ pedicure	**en manikyr/pedikyr**
	ehn ma • nee • _kewr_/pehd ee • _kewr_
a (sports) massage	**(tränings) massage**
	(_trair_ • nihngs •) ma • _sahsh_
a trim, please…	**en klippning, tack…**
	ehn klihp • nihng, tak

Don't cut it too short. **Klipp det inte för kort.**
klihp dee ihn • ter furr koart

Shorter here. **Kortare här.**
koar • ta • rer hair

Do you do...? **Ger ni...?**
yehr nee...

  acupuncture **akupunktur**
a • keu • puhnk • teur

  aromatherapy **aroma-terapi**
a • roa • ma • teh • ra • pee

  oxygen treatment **syrebehandling**
sew • reh • beh • hand • lihng

Is there a sauna? **Finns det bastu?**
fihns dee bas • teu

Spas and wellness centers are becoming increasingly popular. There are many to choose from, both in urban and rural areas. It is possible to find spas that offer everything from traditional massage, such as the Swedish massage, which focuses on circulation and relaxation, to yoga, exercise and more. Some are even eco-friendly. Many spas and health centers also have gyms, pools and saunas.

ANTIQUES

How old is this? **Hur gammalt är det här?**
heur gam • alt air dee hair

Do you have anything from the ... era? **Har ni något från ... perioden?**
hahr nee noh • goht frohn ...
per • eeoh • dehn

Will I have problems with customs? **Får jag problem i tullen?**
foar yahg proa • bleem ee tuh • lehn

Is there a certificate of authenticity?	**Finns det ett äkthetsbevis?**
	fihns dee eht ehkt • heets • beh • vees
Can you ship/wrap it?	**Kan ni skicka/packa in det?**
	kahn nee shih • ka/paka ihn deht

CLOTHING

I'd like...	**Jag skulle vilja ha...**
	yahg skuh • ler vihl • ya hah...
Can I try this on?	**Kan jag prova den här?**
	kan yahg proa • va dehn hair
It doesn't fit.	**Den passar inte.**
	dehn pas • ar ihn • ter
It's too...	**Den är för...**
	dehn air furr...
big	**stor**
	stoar
small	**liten**
	lee • tehn
short	**kort**
	kort
long	**lång**
	loang
tight	**liten**
	leetehn
loose	**stor**
	stohr
Do you have this in size...?	**Har ni den här i storlek...?**
	hahr nee dehn hair ee stoar • leek...
Do you have this in a bigger/smaller size?	**Har ni den här i en större/en mindre storlek?**
	hahr nee dehn hair ee ehn stur • re/ehn mihn • drer stoar • leek

For Numbers, see page 22.

YOU MAY SEE...

HERRKLÄDER	men's clothing
DAMKLÄDER	women's clothing
BARNKLÄDER	children's clothing

YOU MAY HEAR...

Du klär jättebra i den.	That looks great on you.
Deu klair jai • teh • brah i dehn	
Hur sitter den?	How does it fit?
huhr sih • tehr dehn	
Vi har inte din storlek.	We don't have your size.
Vee hahr ihnte deen stohr • lehk	

COLORS

I'm looking for something in...	**Jag söker något i...**
	yahg <u>sur</u> • ker <u>noa</u> • goht ee...
beige	**beige**
	beesh
black	**svart**
	svart
blue	**blått**
	bloat
brown	**brunt**
	*br**eu**nt*
gray	**grått**
	groat

green	**grönt**
	grurnt
orange	**orange**
	oa • <u>ransh</u>
pink	**rosa**
	<u>roa</u> • sa
purple	**lila**
	<u>lee</u> • la
red	**rött**
	ruhrt
white	**vitt**
	vit
yellow	**gult**
	geult
I'm looking for something in…	**Jag söker något i…**
	yahg <u>sur</u> • ker <u>noa</u> • goht ee…

CLOTHES & ACCESSORIES

a backpack	**ryggsäck**
	<u>rewg</u> • sehk
a belt	**skärp**
	shairp
a bikini	**bikini**
	bih • <u>kee</u> • nee
a blouse	**blus**
	bleus
a bra	**behå**
	<u>beh</u> • hoa
briefs [underpants]	**kalsonger [underbyxor]**
	khal • <u>sohn</u> • gehr [uhn • dehr • bew • xohr]
panties	**trosor**
	troh·sohr
a coat	**rock**
	rohk

a dress	**klänning**	
	klehn • ihng	
a hat	**hatt**	
	hat	
a jacket	**jacka**	
	ya • ka	
jeans	**jeans**	
	jeens	
pajamas	**pyjamas**	
	pew • ya • mas	
pants [trousers]	**byxor**	
	bewx • ohr	
panty hose [tights]	**strumpbyxor**	
	struhmp • bewx • ohr	
a purse [handbag]	**handväska**	
	hand • vehs • ka	
a raincoat	**regnkappa**	
	rehngn • kap • a	
a scarf	**halsduk**	
	hals • deuk	
a shirt	**skjorta**	
	shoar • ta	
shorts	**shorts**	
	shohrts	
a skirt	**kjol**	
	choal	
socks	**sockar**	
	soh • kar	
stockings	**strumpor**	
	stuhm • pohr	
a suit (jacket and pants)	**kostym**	
	kos • tewm	
a suit (jacket and skirt)	**dräkt**	
	drehkt	

sunglasses	**solglasögon**
	soal • glahs • _ur_ • gohn
a sweater	**tröja**
	trur • ya
a sweatshirt	**sweatshirt**
	sweat • shirt swimming
swimming trunks	**badbyxor**
	bahd • bewx • ohr
a swimsuit	**baddräkt**
	bahd • drehkt
a T-shirt	**T-skjorta**
	tee • shoarta
a tie	**slips**
	slihps
underpants	**kalsonger/trosor**
(men's/women's)	kal • _soang_ • ehr/_troa_ • sohr
underwear	**underkläder**
	uhn • dehr • klai • dehr

FABRIC

I'd like...	**Jag skulle vilja ha...**
	yahg _skuh_ • ler _vihl_ • ya hah...
cotton	**bomull**
	boam • uhl
denim	**denim**
	dehn • ihm
lace	**spets**
	spehts
leather	**läder**
	lair • der
linen	**linne**
	lih • ner
silk	**siden**
	see • dehn

wool	**ull**
	uhl
Is it machine washable?	**Kan det tvättas i maskin?**
	kan dee tveht•as ee ma•sheen

SHOES

I'd like...	**Jag skulle vilja ha...**
	yahg skuh•ler vihl•ya hah...
high-heeled/ flat shoes	**högklackade/lågklackade skor**
	hurg•klak•a•der/loag•klak•a•der skoar
boots	**stövlar**
	stuhv•lar
I'd like...	**Jag skulle vilja ha...**
	yahg skuh•ler vihl•ya hah...
loafers	**loafers**
	loa•fers
sandals	**sandaler**
	san•dahl•ehr
shoes	**skor**
	skoar
slippers	**tofflor**
	toff•lohr
sneakers	**träningsskor**
	trair•nihngs•skoar
In size...	**I storlek...**
	ee stoar•leek...

For Numbers, see page 22.

SIZES

Small (S)	**liten**
	leet•ehn

Medium (M)	**medium**
	mee • dee • uhm
large (L)	**stor**
	stoar
extra large (XL)	**extra stor**
	ehx • tra stoar
petite	**petite**
	peh • teet
plus size	**plus-storlek**
	pleus • stoar • leek

NEWSAGENT & TOBACCONIST

Do you sell English language books/ newspapers?	**Säljer ni böcker/tidningar på engelska?**
	sehl • yehr nee bur • kehr/teed • nihng • ar poa ehng • ehl • ska
I'd like…	**Jag skulle vilja ha…**
	yahg skuh • ler vihl • ya hah…
candy [sweets]	**godis [sötsaker]**
	goa • dihs [sut • sahk • ehr]
some chewing gum	**tuggummi**
	tuhg • guh • mee
a chocolate bar	**en chokladkaka**
	ehn shohk • lahd • kahka
some cigars	**några cigarrer**
	noa • gra see • gahr • er
a pack/carton of cigarettes	**ett paket/en limpa cigaretter**
	eht pak • eht/ehn lihm • pa sih • ga • reht • her
a lighter	**en tändare**
	ehn tehn • da • rehr
a magazine	**en veckotidning**
	ehn veh • koa • teed • nihng
matches	**tändstickor**
	tehnd • stik • ohr

a newspaper	**en tidning**
	ehn teed • nihng
a pen	**en penna**
	ehn peh • na
a postcard	**ett vykort**
	eht vew • koart
a road/town map of...	**en vägkarta/stadskarta över...**
	ehn vairg • kahr • ta/stats • kahr • ta ur • vehr...
some stamps	**några frimärken**
	noa • gra free • mair • kehn

PHOTOGRAPHY

I'm looking for... camera.	**Jag skulle vilja köpa...kamera.**
	yahg skuh • ler vihl • ya chur • pa... kah • meh • ra
an automatic	**en automatisk**
	ehn ah • toa • mah • tihsk
a digital	**en digital**
	ehn dih • gih • tahl
a disposable	**en engångs**
	ehn een • goangs
I'd like...	**Jag skulle vilja ha...**
	yahg skuh • ler vihl • ya hah...
a battery	**ett batteri**
	eht ba • teh • ree
a digital print	**ett digitalt kort**
	eht dih • gih • tahlt koart
a memory card	**ett minneskort**
	eht mihn • ehs • koart
Can I print digital photos here?	**Kan jag skriva ut digitala foton här?**
	kan yahg skree • va eut dih • gih • tah • la foh • toan hair

SOUVENIRS

candlesticks	**ljusstakar**
	yeus • stah • kar
Christmas	**juldekorationer**
decorations	*yeul • dehk • oh • ra • shoan • ehr*
clogs	**träskor**
	trair • skoar
crystal (glass)	**kristallglas**
	kree • stal • glahs
a Dala horse	**en dalahäst**
(red wooden horse)	*ehn dah • la • hehst*
dolls	**dockor**
	dok • oar
glassware	**glasföremål**
	glahs • furr • reh • moal
handicrafts	**hemslöjd**
	hehm • sluhyd
horn work	**något i horn**
	noa • goht ee hoarn
jewelry	**smycken**
	smew • kehn
porcelain	**porslin**
	pohrsh • leen
pottery	**keramik**
	cheh • ra • meek
reindeer antlers	**renhorn**
	reen • hoarn
Sami handicrafts	**sameslöjd**
	sah • meh • sluhyd
smoked salmon	**rökt lax**
	rurkt lax
a tablecloth	**en duk**
	ehn deuk

textiles	**textil**
	tehx • teel
wood carvings	**träfigurer**
	trair • fih • geu • rehr
a wooden knife	**en träkniv**
	ehn trair • kneev
a wooden spoon	**en träsked**
	ehn trair • sheed
Can I see this/that?	**Får jag se på den här/där?**
	foar yahg she poa
	dehn hair/dair
The one in the window/display case.	**Den i fönstret/vitrinet.**
	dehn ee furn • streht/vi • treen • eht
I'd like…	**Jag skulle vilja ha…**
	yahg skuh • ler vihl • ya hah…
a battery	**ett batteri**
	eht ba • teh • ree
a bracelet	**ett armband**
	eht arm • band
a brooch	**en brosch**
	ehn broash
earrings	**örhängen**
	ur • hehng • ehn
a necklace	**ett halsband**
	eht hals • band
a ring	**en ring**
	ehn rihng
a watch	**en armbandsklocka**
	ehn arm • bands • kloh • ka
copper	**koppar**
	kohpp • ar
crystal (quartz)	**kristall**
	krihs • tall

(i)

When it comes to souvenirs, whether you are looking for something traditional or modern, you are sure to find just the thing in Sweden. **Träslöjd** (woodwork), **hemslöjd** (handicrafts), **keramik** (ceramics) and Swedish crystal are popular, traditional souvenirs. The **dalahäst** (Dala horse) is perhaps one of the most famous and ubiquitous souvenirs; traditionally, its color is a reddish-orange, but the horses can now be found in a wide range of colors and sizes. Sweden is known for its design, which is evident in its selection of **porslin** (fine china) and ceramics. Some well-known manufacturers include **Höganäs Keramik** and **Rörstrand**, the latter being the second oldest porcelain manufacturer in Europe, founded in 1746. Sweden is also famous for its glass and crystal, both with respect to design and to quality. **Glasriket** (the kingdom of glass) located in Småland, in southeastern Sweden, has around 15 glass factories, including some of the most famous glassworks in Sweden, such as **Kosta Boda**, **Orrefors** and **Nybro**. Factory tours are often available. In addition to the traditional Swedish handicrafts mentioned above, **sameslöjd** (Sámi handicraft) is something that should not be overlooked. The **Sámi** are known for their beautiful crafts, which include jewelry and knives carved from reindeer antlers, jewelry made from beaded pewter and reindeer leather as well as a wide range of clothing in reindeer leather and different types of fur.

diamond	**diamant**
	dee • a • mant
white/yellow gold	**vitt/rött guld**
	viht/rurtt geuld

pearl	**pärla**
	pair • la
I'd like…	**Jag skulle vilja ha…**
	yahg skuh • ler vihl • ya hah…
pewter	**tenn**
	teen
platinum	**platina**
	plah • tee • na
sterling silver	**äkta silver**
	ehk • ta sihl • vehr
Is this real?	**Är den här äkta?**
	air dehn hair ehk • ta
Can you engrave it?	**Kan ni gravera den?**
	kan nee gra • vee • ra dehn

SPORT & LEISURE

NEED TO KNOW

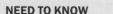

When's the game?	**När börjar matchen?**
	nair bur • yar ma • shchehn
Where's…?	**Var ligger…?**
	vahr lih • gehr…
the beach	**stranden**
	stran • dehn
Where's…?	**Var ligger…?**
	vahr lih • gehr…
the park	**parken**
	park • ehn
the pool	**simbassängen**
	sihm • ba • sehng • ehn

Is it safe to swim/ dive here?	**Kan man simma/dyka här utan risk?**
	kan man sihmm•a/dew•ka hair eu•tan rihsk
Can I rent [hire] golf clubs?	**Kan man hyra golfklubbor?**
	kan man hew•ra gohlf•kluh•bohr
How much per hour?	**Vad kostar det per timme?**
	vahd kos•tar dee pair tihm•er
How far is it to...?	**Hur långt är det till...?**
	heur loangt air dee tihl...
Can you show me on the map?	**Kan du visa mig på kartan?**
	kan deu vee sa may poa kahr•tan

WATCHING SPORT

When's...?	**När börjar...?**
	nair bur•yar...
the baseball game	**basebollmatchen**
	base•bohl•mat•shehn
the basketball game	**basketbollmatchen**
	bahs•keht•bohl•ma•shchehn

(i)

Sports and recreation are popular, and there are excellent sports facilities everywhere, ranging from **golf** (golf), **fiske** (fishing), **tennis** (tennis) and **fotboll** (soccer) to **skidåkning** (skiing) and **ishockey** (ice hockey). Tourist offices should have contact information for the various sports facilities in your area. Swedes also love the great outdoors, and the country has much to offer when it comes to **bergklättring** (mountain climbing), **vandring** (hiking), **ridsport** (horsebackriding), **cykelåkning** (cycling), **paddla kanot** (canoeing) and **segling** (boating). Whether you are looking for a day hike or planning a longer trip, some great choices include **Kebnekaise**, which is Sweden's highest mountain, **Kungsleden**, **Bohusleden** or **Padjelantleden**. There are a lot of options for cyclists, both amateurs and professionals, and popular cycle routes include **Kustlinjen** and **Sverigeleden**.

the boxing match	**boxningsmatchen**
	boax • nihngs • matsh • ehn
the cricket game	**cricketspelet**
	cricket • matsh • ehn
the cycling race	**cykeltävlingen**
	sew • kehl • taiv • lihng • ehn
the golf	**golfspelet**
tournament	*golf • spee • leht*
the soccer	**fotbollsmatchen**
[football] game	*foat • bohls • ma • shchehn*
the tennis match	**tennismatchen**
	tehn • ihs • ma • shchehn
the volleyball game	**volleybollspelet**
	voh • lee • bohl • spee • leht

Which teams are playing?	**Vilka lag spelar?**
	vihl • ka lahg spee • lar
Where's the stadium?	**Var ligger idrottsarenan?**
	vahr lih • gehr ee • drohts • a • ree • nan
Where's the horsetrack/racetrack?	**Var finns hästkapplöpnings/kapplöpningsbanan?**
	Vahr fihns hehst • kap • luhp • nihngs/kahp • luhp • nihgs • bahn • an
Where can I place a bet?	**Var kan jag spela lotto?**
	vahr kan yahg spee • la loh • toa

PLAYING SPORT

Is there…nearby?	**Finns det…i närheten?**
	fihns dee…ee nair • hee • ten
a golf course	**en golfbana**
	ehn gohlf • bah • na
a gym	**ett gym**
	eht yim
a park	**en park**
	ehn park
a tennis court	**en tennisbana**
	ehn tehn • ihs • bah • nohr
How much per…?	**Hur mycket kostar det per…?**
	heur mew • ker kos • tar dee pair…
day	**dag**
	dahg
hour	**timme**
	tihm • er
game	**spel**
	speel
round	**runda**
	ruhn • da
Can I rent [hire]…?	**Kan man hyra…?**
	kan man hew • ra…

golf clubs	**klubbor**
	kluhb • ohr
equipment	**utrustning**
	eut • ruhst • nihng
a racket	**en racket**
	ehn ra • keht

AT THE BEACH/POOL

Where's the beach/pool?	**Var är stranden/simbassängen?**
	vahr air stran • dehn/ sihm • ba • sehng • ehn
Is there a…here?	**Finns det…här?**
	fihns dee…hair
a kiddie [paddling] pool	**en barnbassäng**
	ehn bahrn • bah • sehng
an indoor/outdoor pool	**en inomhuspool/utomhuspool**
	ehn in • ohm • heus • poal/ eut • ohm • heus • poal
a lifeguard	**en livräddare**
	leev • rehd • a • rer
Is it safe to swim/dive?	**Kan man simma/dyka här utan risk?**
	Kan man sihm • a/dew • ka hair eu • tan rihsk
Is it safe for children?	**Är det barnsäkert?**
	air dee bahrn • sair • kert
I want to hire…	**Jag skulle vilja hyra…**
	yahg skuh • ker vihl • ya hew • ra…
a deck chair	**en solstol**
	ehn soal • stoal
diving equipment	**dykutrustning**
	dewk • uht • ruhst • nihng
a jet ski	**en jetski**
	ehn jeht • skee

a motorboat	**en motorbåt**
	ehn <u>moa</u> • tor • boat
a rowboat	**en roddbåt**
	ehn <u>rohd</u> • boat
snorkeling	**snorklingsutrustning**
equipment	*snoh • rklihngs • uht • ruhst • nihng*
a surfboard	**en surfbräda**
	ehn <u>suhrf</u> • brair • da
a towel	**en handduk**
	ehn <u>hand</u> • deuk
an umbrella	**en solparasol**
	ehn <u>soal</u> • pa • ra • <u>sohl</u>
water skis	**vattenskidor**
	<u>va</u> • tehrn • shee • dohr
a windsurfer	**en vindsurfare**
	ehn vihnd • suhr • fa • reh

For Traveling with Children, see page 134.

For Traveling with Children, see page 134.

(i)

A significant portion of the Swedish coastline is rough, covered with granite rocks and cliffs and dotted with beaches. Most of the sandy beaches are found in the south and on the southwest coasts. Around Stockholm you can swim and dive from the small islands in the archipelago — and you can even swim in the water around Stockholm itself. Inland lakes, coastal areas and the popular archipelagos of Stockholm and the West Coast are perfect for boaters, and canoeists and kayakers alike.

WINTER SPORTS

A lift pass for a day/ five days, please.	**Ett liftpass för en dag/för fem dagar, tack.**
	eht lihft • pas furr ehn dahg/furr fehm dahg • ar tak
Where's the ice rink?	**Var ligger isbanan?**
	vahr lee • gehr ihs • bahn • an
Are there lessons?	**Kan man få lektioner?**
	kan man foa lehk • shoa • nehr
How much?	**Hur mycket?**
	huhr mew • keh
I'm a beginner.	**Jag är nybörjare.**
	yahg air new • bur • yah • reh
I'm experienced.	**Jag har erfarenhet.**
	yahg hahr air • fah • rehn • heet

Swedes grow up with skiing: cross-country in the south and downhill in the north. There are many excellent ski resorts in the north, offering superb skiing and first-class facilities. Many hotels offer three- to seven-day package deals, including transportation and accommodation. In June, try **Riksgränsen** for a taste of skiing in the midnight sun.

Långfärdsbussar (long-distance buses) are efficient, relatively cheap and run daily to all major towns and resorts. Most of the major ski resorts also offer other winter sport activities like snowmobile safaris, snowshoeing and dog sledding tours. **Ishotellet** (Ice Hotel), though not a ski resort specifically, does offer several of these activities.

I'd like to hire…	**Jag skulle vilja hyra…**
	yahg <u>skuh</u> • ler <u>vihl</u> • ya <u>hew</u> • ra…
boots	**skidpjäxor**
	<u>sheed</u> • pyeaix • ohr
a helmet	**en hjälm**
	ehn yehlm
ice skates	**skridskor**
	skrih • skohr
poles	**stavar**
	<u>stah</u> • var
skis	**skidor**
	<u>shee</u> • dohr
a snowboard	**en snowboard**
	ehn <u>snow</u> • board
snowshoes	**pjäxor**
	<u>pyaix</u> • ohr
These are too big/small.	**De här är för stora/små.**
	dehm hair air furr <u>stoa</u> • ra/sm<u>oa</u>
A trail [piste] map, please.	**En karta över spåren, tack.**
	ehn <u>kahr</u> • ta <u>ur</u> • vehr <u>spoa</u> • rehn tak

---

YOU MAY SEE…

DRAGLIFT	drag lift
ÄGGLIFT	cable car
STOLLIFT	chair lift
NYBÖRJARE	novice
MELLANNIVÅ	intermediate
AVANCERAD	expert
SPÅRET STÄNGD	trail [piste]
	closed

OUT IN THE COUNTRY

I'd like a map of…	**Jag skulle vilja ha en karta över…** *yahg <u>skuh</u> • ler <u>vihl</u> • ya hah ehn <u>kahr</u> • ta <u>ur</u> • vehr…*
this region	**denna region** *<u>dehn</u> • a reh • <u>gioan</u>*
walking routes	**vandringsleder** *<u>van</u> • drihngs • <u>lee</u> • dehr*
cycle routes	**cykeleder** *<u>sew</u> • kehl • <u>lee</u> • dehr*
the trails	**spåren** *s<u>poa</u> • rehn*
Is it easy/difficult?	**Är det lätt/svårt?** *air d<u>ee</u> leht/sv<u>oa</u>rt*
Is it far/steep?	**Är det långt/brant?** *air d<u>ee</u> l<u>oa</u>ngt/brant*
How far is it to…?	**Hur långt är det till…?** *heur <u>loa</u>ngt air d<u>ee</u> tihl…*
Can you show me on the map?	**Kan du visa mig på kartan?** *kan deu <u>vee</u> • sa may p<u>oa</u> <u>kahr</u> • tan*
I'm lost.	**Jag har kommit vilse.** *yahg hahr <u>koh</u> • miht <u>vihl</u> • ser*

Where's...?	**Var ligger...?**
	vahr <u>lih</u> • gehr...
the bridge	**bron**
	broan
the cave	**grottan**
	<u>*groht*</u> • *an*
the cliff	**klippa**
	<u>*klihp*</u> • *an*
the farm	**bondgården**
	<u>*boand*</u> • *g***oa***rd* • *ehn*
the field	**åkern**
	oak • *ern*
the footpath	**fotvandringsleden**
	<u>*foat*</u> • *vand* • *rihngs* • <u>*lee*</u> • *dehn*
the forest	**skogen**
	<u>*sk***oa***g*</u> • *ehn*
the hill	**berget**
	behr • *yeht*
the lake	**sjön**
	*sh***ur***n*
the mountain	**berget**
	<u>*behr*</u> • *yeht*
the mountain pass	**bergspasset**
	<u>*berys*</u> • *pas* • *eht*
the mountain range	**bergskedjan**
	<u>*berys*</u> • *chee* • *dyan*
the nature reserve	**naturreservatet**
	na • <u>*teur*</u> • *res* • *her* • <u>*vah*</u> • *teht*
the panorama	**panoraman**
	pan • *o* • <u>*rah*</u> • *man*
the park	**parken**
	<u>*park*</u> • *ehn*
the path	**stigen**
	stee • *gehn*

Where's…?	**Var ligger…?**
	vahr lih•gehr…
the peak	**toppen**
	tohp•ehn
the picnic area/	**picknickområdet/rastplatsen**
rest area	*pihk•nihk•ohm•roa•det/*
	rast•plats•ehn
the pond	**dammen**
	dah•mehn
the river	**floden**
	fload•ehn
the sea	**havet**
	hafv•eht
the hot spring	**den varma källan**
	dehn var•ma cheh•lan
the valley	**dalen**
	dahl•ehn
the viewpoint	**utsiktspunkten**
	eut•sihkts•peunk•tehn
the village	**byn**
	bewn
the vineyard	**vinodlingen**
	vihn•ohd•lihng•ehn
the waterfall	**vattenfallet**
	va•tehrn•fal

TRAVELING WITH CHILDREN

NEED TO KNOW

Is there a discount for kids?	**Har ni barnrabatt?**
	hahr nee bahrn•rah•bat
Can you recommend a babysitter?	**Kan du rekommendera en barnvakt?**
	kan deu reh•koh•mehn•dee•ra ehn bahrn•vakt
Could I have a highchair?	**Kan jag få en barnstol, tack?**
	kan yahg foa ehn bahrn•stoal tak
Where can I change the baby?	**Var kan jag byta på babyn?**
	vahr kan yahg bew•ta poa bai•been
Where's...?	**Var ligger...?**
	vahr lih•gehr...
the amusement park	**nöjesfältet**
	nury•ehs•fehl•teht
the arcade	**arkadhallen**
	ar•kahd•ha•lehn
the kiddie [paddling] pool	**barnbassängen**
	bahrn•ba•sehng•ehn
the park	**parken**
	park•kehn
the playground	**lekplatsen**
	leek•plats•ehn
the zoo	**djurparken**
	yeur•park•ehn
Are kids allowed?	**Får man ta barnen med?**
	foar man tah bahr•nehn meed
Is it safe for kids?	**Är det barnsäkert?**
	air det bahrn•sair•kert

YOU MAY HEAR...

Vad gullig!
vahd geul • ig

How cute!

Vad heter han/hon?
vahd hee • tehr han/hoan

What's his/her name?

Hur gammal är han/hon?
heur gam • al air han/hoan

How old is he/she?

OUT & ABOUT

Can you recommend something for kids?	**Kan du föreslå något för barn?** *kan deu furr • reh • sloa noa • goht furr bahrn*
Where's...?	**Var är...?** *Vahr air...*
the amusement park	**nöjesparken** *nuy • ehs • pahr • kehn*
the arcade	**gallerian** *gah • le • ree • an*
the kiddie [paddling] pool	**barnbassängen/plaskdammen** *bah • rn • ba • sehng • ehn/ plask • da • mehn*
the park	**parken** *par • kehn*
the playground	**lekplatsen** *lehk • plat • sehn*
the zoo	**djurparken** *yeur • par • kehn*
Are kids allowed?	**Tillåts barn?** *tihl • oats bahrn*
Is it safe for kids?	**Är det säkert för barn?** *air deht seh • kehrt furr bahrn*

| Is it suitable for… year olds? | **Passar det för…-åringar?** |
| | _pas • ar dee furr…__oa__ • rihng • ar_ |

For Numbers, see page 22.

BABY ESSENTIALS

Do you have…?	**Har ni…?**
	hahr nee…
a baby bottle	**en nappflaska**
	_ehn __nap__ • flas • ka_
baby food	**babymat**
	behy • bih • maht
baby wipes	**våtservetter för barn**
	_voat • ser • __veht__ • er furrbahrn_
a car seat	**en bilbarnstol**
	_ehn __beel__ • bahrn • stoal_
a children's menu	**en barnmeny**
	_ehn bahrn • meh • __new___
a children's portion	**en barnportion**
	_bahrn • pohrt • __shoan___
a highchair	**en barnstol**
	_ehn __bahrn__ • stoal_

a crib	**en barnsäng**
	ehn <u>bahrn</u> • sehng
diapers [nappies]	**blöjor**
	<u>blury</u> • ohr
formula	**välling**
	<u>vehl</u> • ihng
a pacifier [dummy]	**en napp**
	ehn nap
a playpen	**ett lekrum**
	eht <u>leek</u> • ruhm
a stroller	**en sittvagn**
[pushchair]	*ehn <u>siht</u> • vangn*
Can I breastfeed the	**Får jag amma barnet här?**
baby here?	*foar yahg ah • ma bahr • neht hair*
Where can I change	**Var kan jag byta på babyn?**
the baby?	*vahr kan yahg <u>bew</u> • ta poa <u>bai</u> • been*

For Dining with Children, see page 168.

BABYSITTING

Can you recommend	**Kan du rekommendera en pålitlig**
a reliable babysitter?	**barnvakt?**
	kaun deu re • koh • mehn • <u>dee</u> • rahra
	ehn poa • <u>leet</u> • lihg bahrn • vakt
What's the charge?	**Vad kostar det?**
	vahd <u>kos</u> • tar dee
We'll be back by...	**Vi kommer tillbaka**
	Vee koh • mehr tihl • bah • ka
I'll pick them up at...	**Jag hämtar dem...**
	yahg <u>hehm</u> • tar dehm...
I can be reached at...	**Du kan nå mig på...**
	deu kan noa may poa...

For Time, see page 24

HEALTH & SAFETY

EMERGENCIES

NEED TO KNOW

Help!	**Hjälp!**
	yelp
Go away!	**Ge er iväg!**
	yeh ehr ee • vairg
Stop thief!	**Stoppa tjuven!**
	stop • a shcheu • vehn
Get a doctor!	**Hämta en läkare!**
	hehm • ta ehn lair • ka • rer
Fire!	**Det brinner!**
	dee brihn • ehr
I'm lost.	**Jag har gått vilse.**
	yahg hahr goat vihl • ser
Can you help me?	**Kan du hjälpa mig?**
	kan deu yehl • pa may

YOU MAY HEAR...

Fyll i blanketten, tack.
fewl ee blan • keht • ehn tak

Er legitimation, tack.
ehr lehg • ee • tih • ma • shoan tak

När/Var hände det?
nair/vahr hehn • dehr dee

Hur ser han/hon ut?
hewr seer han/hoan eut

Please fill out this form.

Your identification, please.

When/Where did it happen?

What does he/she look like?

In an emergency, dial: **112**.
This number will connect you to the police, the fire brigade or an ambulance.

POLICE

NEED TO KNOW

Call the police!	**Ring polisen!**
	rihng poa • lee • sehn
Where's the nearest police station?	**Var ligger närmaste polisstation?**
	vahr lih • gehr nair • mas • ter poo • lees • sta • shoan
There's been an accident.	**Det har hänt en olycka.**
	det hahr hehnt ehn oa • lewk • a
I've been attacked.	**Jag har blivit anfallen.**
	jahg hahr blee • viht an • fa • lehn
My child is missing.	**Mitt barn har kommit bort.**
	miht bahrn hahr koh • miht bohrt
I need...	**Jag behöver...**
	yahg beh • hur • vehr...
an interpreter	**en tolk**
	ehn tohlk
to contact my lawyer	**kontakta min advokat**
	kohn • tak • ta mihn ad • voh • kaht
to make a phone call	**ringa ett samtal**
	rihng • a eht sam • tahl
I'm innocent.	**Jag är oskyldig.**
	yahg air oa • shewl • dihg

CRIME & LOST PROPERTY

I want to report...	**Jag vill anmäla...**
	yahg vihl <u>an</u> • mair • la...
a mugging	**ett överfall**
	eht <u>ur</u> • vehr • fal
a rape	**en våldtäkt**
	ehn <u>vohld</u> • tehkt
a theft	**ett rån**
	eht roan
I've been robbed/ mugged.	**Jag har blivit rånad/överfallen.**
	yahg hahr <u>blee</u> • viht roa • nad/ <u>ur</u> • veh • fal • ehn
I've lost...	**Jag har tappet...**
	yahg hahr <u>tah</u> • pat...
My...has been stolen.	**Någon har stulit...**
	<u>noa</u> • gohn hahr <u>steu</u> • liht...
backpack	**min ryggsäck**
	mihn <u>rewg</u> • sehk
bicycle	**min cykel**
	mihn <u>sew</u> • kehl
camera	**min kamera**
	mihn <u>kah</u> • meh • ra

rental car	**min bil/hyrbil**
	mihn beel/<u>hewr</u> • beel
computer	**min dator**
	mihn <u>dah</u> • tohr
credit cards	**mina kreditkort**
	mee • na kre • <u>deet</u> • koart
jewelry	**mina smycken**
	mee • na <u>smew</u> • ken
money	**mina pengar**
	mee • na <u>pehng</u> • ar
passport	**mitt pass**
	miht pas
purse [handbag]	**min portmonnä**
	mihn pohrt • mo • <u>nai</u>
traveler's checks [cheques]	**mina resecheckar**
	<u>mee</u> • na <u>ree</u> • seh • shehk • ar
wallet	**min plånbok**
	mihn <u>ploan</u> • boak
I need a police report for my insurance.	**Jag behöver en polisanmälan till min försäkring.**
	yahg beh • hu • vehr ehn poal • ees • an • mailan tihl meen furr • sehk·rihng
Where is the British/American/Irish embassy?	**Var ligger den brittiska/amerikanska ambassaden?**
	var ligger den brittiska/amerikanska ambassaden?

HEALTH

NEED TO KNOW

I'm sick [ill].	**Jag är sjuk.**
	yahg air sheuk
I need an English-speaking doctor.	**Jag behöver en engelsktalande läkare.**
	yahg beh • hur • vehr ehn ehng • ehlsk • tahl • an • der lair • ka • rer
It hurts here.	**Det gör ont här.**
	dee yurr oant hair
I have a stomachache.	**Jag har ont i magen.**
	yahg hahr oant ee mah • gehn

FINDING A DOCTOR

Can you recommend a doctor/dentist?	**Kan du rekommendera en läkare/tandläkare?**
	kan deu reh • koh • mehn • dee • ra ehn lair • ka • rer/tand • lair • ka • rer
Can the doctor come to see me here?	**Kan doktorn komma och undersöka mig här?**
	kan dohk • torn koh • ma ohk eun • der • sur • ka may hair
I need an English-speaking doctor.	**Jag behöver en engelsktalande läkare.**
	yahg beh • uv • ehr en eeng • ehlsk • tah • lan • de leh • ka • re
What are their office hours?	**Vilka är deras öppettider?**
	vihl • ka air dee • ras ur • peh • tee • dehr

HJÄLPTELEFON

RIKSPOLISSTYRELSEN

Can I make an appointment for…?	**Kan jag boka en tid…?**
	kan yahg <u>boa</u> • ka ehn teed…
today	**idag**
	ee • dahg
tomorrow	**imorgon**
	ee • mo • ron
as soon as possible	**så snart som möjligt**
	soa snahrt som <u>mury</u> • ligt
It's urgent.	**Det är brådskande.**
	dee air <u>broas</u> • kan • der

SYMPTOMS

I'm…	**Jag…**
	yahg…
bleeding	**blöder**
	<u>blur</u> • dehr
constipated	**är förstoppad**
	air furr • <u>stop</u> • ad
dizzy	**har yrsel**
	hahr <u>ewr</u> • sehl
nauseous	**mår illa**
	moar <u>ihl</u> • la

vomiting	**kräks**	
	krairks	
It hurts here.	**Det gör ont här.**	
	dee yurr oant hair	
I have...	**Jag har...**	
	yahg hahr...	
an allergic	**en allergisk reaktion**	
reaction	*ehn a • lehr • gihsk ree • ak • shoan*	
chest pain	**ont i bröstet**	
	oant ee brurs • teht	
cramps	**kramper**	
	kram • pehr	
diarrhea	**diarré**	
	dee • ar • ee	
an earache	**ont i örat**	
	oant ee ur • rat	
a fever	**feber**	
	fee • behr	
pain	**ont**	
	oant	
a rash	**ett utslag**	
	eht eut • slahg	
a sprain	**en stukning**	
	ehn steuk • nihng	
some swelling	**en lätt svullnad**	
	ehn leht sveul • nad	
a stomachache	**ont i magen**	
	oant ee mah • gehn	
sunstroke	**solsting**	
	soal • stihng	
I've been sick [ill]	**Jag har varit sjuk i...dagar.**	
for...days.	*yahg hahr vah • riht sheuk ee...dah • gar*	

For Numbers, see page 22.

YOU MAY HEAR...

Vad är det för fel?	What's wrong?
vahd air dee fur feel	
Var gör det ont?	Where does it
vahr yur dee oant	hurt?
Gör det ont här?	Does it hurt
yur deht ohnt hehr	here?
Tar du någon annan medicin?	Are you taking
tahr deu noa • gohn an • an	any other
meh • dih • seen	medication?
Är du allergisk mot något?	Are you allergic
air deu a • lehr • gihsk moat noa • goht	to anything?
Öppna munnen.	Open your
urp • na muhn • ehn	mouth.
Andas djupt.	Breathe deeply.
an • das yeupt	
Hosta, tack.	Cough, please.
hoas • ta, tak	
Du behöver åka till sjukhuset.	You need to go
deu beh • hur • vehr oa • ka tihl	to the
sjeuk • heu • seht	hospital.

CONDITIONS

I'm anemic/diabetic.	**Jag är anemisk/diabetiker.**
	yahg air a • nee • mihsk/
	dee • a • beh • tih • ker
I'm epileptic.	**Jag har epilepsi.**
	yahg hahr eh • pih • leh • psi

I'm allergic to antibiotics/ penicillin.	**Jag är allergisk mot antibiotika/ penicillin.**
	yahg air a • lehr • gihsk moat an • tih • bee • oa • tee • ka/ pehn • eh • si • leen
I have...	**Jag har...**
	yahg hahr...
arthritis	**artrit**
	ar • treet
asthma	**astma**
	as • ma
high/low blood pressure	**högt/låg blodtryck**
	hurgt/loagt bload • trewk
a heart condition	**hjärtproblem**
	yairt • proa • bleem
I'm taking... (medicine).	**Jag tar...(medicin).**
	yahg tahr...(meh • dee • seen)

TREATMENT

Can you prescribe a generic drug [unbranded medication]?	**Kan du skriva ut ett generiskt läkemedel [generika]?**
	Kahn deu skrih • va eut eht gehn • eh • rih • skt lai • keh • meh • dehl [gehn • eh • rih • ka]
Where can I get it?	**Var hittar jag det?**
	vahr hih • tar yahg deht
Do I need a prescription/ medicine?	**Behöver jag ett recept/medicin?**
	beh • hur • vehr yahg eht reh • sehpt/ meh • dih • sihn

For Pharmacy, see page 151.

HOSPITAL

Please notify my family.	**Var snäll och underrätta min familj** *vahr snehl ohk <u>eun</u> • der • rehta mihn <u>fa</u> • mily*
I'm in pain.	**Jag har ont** *yahg hahr oant*
I need a doctor/nurse.	**Jag behöver en läkare/sjuksköterska.** *yahg beh • <u>hur</u> • vehr ehn <u>lair</u> • ka • rer/ sheuk • <u>shur</u> • ter • ska*
When are visiting hours?	**När är det besökstid?** *nair air dee beh • <u>surks</u> • teed*
I'm visiting…	**Jag vill besöka…** *yahg vihl beh • <u>sur</u> • ka…*

DENTIST

I've broken a tooth/lost a filling.	**Jag har brutit av en tand/tappat en plomb.** *yahg hahr <u>breu</u> • tiht afv ehn tand/<u>tap</u> • at ehn plohmb*
This tooth hurts.	**Den här tanden gör ont.** *dehn hair <u>tan</u> • dehn yur oant*
Can you fix this denture?	**Kan du reparera den här tandprotesen?** *kan deu reh • pa • <u>ree</u> • ra dehn hair <u>tand</u> • proh • <u>tees</u> • ehn*

GYNECOLOGIST

I have menstrual cramps/a vaginal infection.	**Jag har mens värk/en vaginal infektion.** *yahg hahr mens vehrk/ehn va • gih • <u>nahl</u> ihn • fehk • <u>shoan</u>*
I missed my period.	**Min mens har inte kommit.** *mihn mehns hahr <u>ihn</u> • ter <u>koh</u> • miht*

I'm on the Pill.	**Jag tar p-piller.**
	yahg tahr pee • pihl • ler
I'm (…months) pregnant.	**Jag är (…månader) gravid.**
	Yahg air (…moh • na • dehr) gra • veed
I'm (not) pregnant.	**Jag är (inte) gravid.**
	yahg air (ihn • ter) gra • veed
I haven't had my period for…months.	**Jag har inte haft mens på… månader.**
	yahg hahr ihn • ter haft mehns poa… moa • na • dehr

For Numbers, see page 22.

OPTICIAN

I've lost…	**Jag har tappat…**
	yahg hahr tap • at…
a contact lens	**en kontaktlins**
	ehn kohn • takt • lihns
my glasses	**mina glasögon**
	mee • na glahs • ur • gohn
a lens	**en lins**
	ehn lihns

PAYMENT & INSURANCE

How much does it cost?	**Hur mycket kostar det?**
	heur mew • ker kos • tar dee
Can I pay by credit card?	**Kan jag betala med kreditkort?**
	kan yahg beh • tah • la meed kreh • deet • koart
I have insurance.	**Jag har försäkring.**
	yahg hahr furr • sair • krihng

Can I have a receipt for my insurance?	**Kan jag få ett kvitto för mitt försäkringsbolag?**
	kan yahg foa eht kvih • toh furr miht furr • sair • krihngs • boa • lahg

PHARMACY

NEED TO KNOW

Where's the nearest pharmacy?	**Var är närmaste apotek?**
	vahr air nair • mas • teh a • poa • teek
What time does the pharmacy open/ close?	**När öppnar/stänger apoteket?**
	nair urp • nar/ stehng • ehr a • poa • tee • keht
What would you recommend for...?	**Vad kan du rekommendera för...?**
	vahd kan deu reh • koh • mehn • dee • ra furr...
How much should I take?	**Hur mycket ska jag ta?**
	heur mew • ker skah yahg tah
Can you fill [make up] this prescription for me?	**Kan ni göra iordning det här receptet åt mig?**
	kan nee yur • ra ee oard • nihng dee hair reh • sehp • teht oat may
I'm allergic to...	**Jag är allergisk mot...**
	yahg air a • lehr • gihsk moat...

WHAT TO TAKE

How much should I take?	**Hur mycket ska jag ta?**
	heur mew • ker skah yahg tah

How many times a day should I take it?	**Hur många gånger om dagen ska jag ta det?**
	heur <u>moang</u>•a <u>goang</u>•er ohm <u>dah</u>•gehn skah yahg tah dee
Is it suitable for children?	**Är det lämpligt för barn?**
	air dee <u>lehmp</u>•lihgt furr bahrn
I'm taking… (medicine).	**Jag tar…(medicin).**
	yahg tahr…(meh•dee•<u>seen</u>)
Are there side effects?	**Ger det några biverkningar?**
	yehr dee noa•gra <u>bee</u>•vehrk•nihng•ar
I'd like some medicine for…	**Jag behöver medicin mot…**
	yahg beh•<u>hur</u>•vehr meh•dih•<u>seen</u> moat…
a cold	**en förkylning**
	ehn furr•<u>chewl</u>•nihng
a cough	**hosta**
	<u>hoas</u>•ta
diarrhea	**diarré**
	dee•a•<u>reh</u>
a headache	**huvudvärk**
	huh•vuhd•vairk
an insect bite	**ett insektbett**
	eht in•<u>sekt</u>•beht
motion sickness	**åksjuka**
	<u>oak</u>•sheu•ka
a sore throat	**halsont**
	<u>hals</u>•oant
a sunburn	**solbränna**
	<u>soal</u>•brehn•a
a toothache	**tandvärk**
	tand•vairk
an upset stomach	**ont i magen**
	oant ee <u>mah</u>•gehn

In addition to filling prescriptions, **apotek** (pharmacies) sell over-the-counter medication as well as their own brands of toiletries and cosmetics. Almost all pharmacies are open on weekdays, but not all are open late in the evening or on weekends. Business hours vary considerably depending on the pharmacy. Generally, business hours are between 9:00 a.m. and 5:00 p.m. on weekdays. Pharmacies that are open in the evening usually close around 9:00 p.m., and weekend hours are generally from 10:00 a.m. to 4:00 p.m.

YOU MAY SEE...

EN GÅNG/TRE GÅNGER PER DAG	once/three times a day
TABLETTER	tablets
DROPPAR TESKEDAR	drop teaspoons
FÖRE/EFTER/TILLSAMMANS MED MÅLTIDER	before/after/ with meals
PÅ FASTANDE MAGE	on an empty stomach
SVÄLJS HELA	swallow whole
KAN ORSAKA DÅSIGHET	may cause drowsiness
ENDAST FÖR UTVÄRTES BRUK	for external use only

BASIC SUPPLIES

I'd like…	**Jag skulle vilja ha…**
	yahg <u>skuh</u> • ler <u>vihl</u> • ya hah…
acetaminophen	**acetominofen**
[paracetamol]	*a • seht • a • mihn • oa • <u>fehn</u>*
antiseptic cream	**antiseptisk salva**
	an • tih • <u>sehp</u> • tihsk sal • va
aspirin	**huvudvärkstabletter**
	<u>heu</u> • vuhd • vairks • ta • <u>bleh</u> • ter
bandage [plasters]	**gasbinda**
	<u>gahs</u> • bihn • da
a comb	**kam**
	kam
condoms	**kondomer**
	kohn • <u>doa</u> • mehr
contact lens	**kontaktlinsvätska**
solution	*kohn • <u>takt</u> • lins • veht • ska*
deodorant	**deodorant**
	dee • oa • deh • <u>rant</u>
a hairbrush	**en hårborste**
	ehn <u>hoar</u> • bohrsh • ter
hair spray	**hårspray**
	<u>hoar</u> • spray
ibuprofen	**ibuprofen**
	ee • beu • proa • <u>fehn</u>
insect repellent	**myggolja**
	<u>mewg</u> • ohl • ya
a nail file	**en nagelfil**
	ehn <u>nah</u> • gehl • feel
a (disposable)	**en (engångs)-rakhyvel**
razor	*ehn (<u>een</u> • goangs) • rahk • <u>hew</u> • vehl*
razor blades	**rakblad**
	<u>rahk</u> • blahd

sanitary napkins [towels]	**bindor** *bin • dohr*
shampoo/	**schampo** *sham • poa*
conditioner	**hårbalsam** *hoar • bal • sam*
soap	**tvål** *tvoal*
sunscreen	**solskyddskräm** *soal • shewds • krairm*
tampons	**tamponger** *tam • poang • ehr*
tissue	**papper näsdukar** *pa • pehrs • nairs • deu • kar*
toilet paper	**toalettpapper** *toa • a • leht • pa • pehr*
a toothbrush	**tandborste** *tand • bohr • ster*
toothpaste	**tandkräm** *tand • krairm*

For Baby Essentials, see page 136.

CHILD HEALTH & EMERGENCY

Can you recommend a pediatrician?	**Kan du rekommendera en barnläkare?** *kan deu reh • koh • men • dee • ra ehn bahrn • lairk • a • rer*
My child is allergic to...	**Mitt barn är allergiskt mot...** *miht bahrn air a • lehr • gisk moat...*
My child is missing.	**Mitt barn har kommit bort.** *miht bahrn hahr koh • miht bohrt*
Have you seen a boy/girl?	**Har du sett en pojke/flicka?** *hahr deu seht ehn poy • ker/flih • ka*

DISABLED TRAVELERS

NEED TO KNOW

Is there...?	**Finns det...?**
	fihns det...
access for the	**ingång för rörelsehindrade**
	in • goang furr
disabled	*rur • rehl • seh • hihn • dra • der*
a wheelchair ramp	**en rullstolsramp**
	ehn reul • stoals • ramp
a handicapped-	**en handikappanpassad toalett**
[disabled-]	*ehn hand • ee • kap • an • pas • ad*
accessible toilet	*toa • ah • leht*
I need...	**Jag behöver...**
	yahg beh • hur • ver...
assistance	**hjälp**
	yehlp
an elevator [lift]	**en hiss**
	ehn hihs
a ground floor	**ett rum på bottenvåningen**
room	*eht ruhm poa*
	boh • tehrn • voa • nihng • hen

ASKING FOR ASSISTANCE

I'm disabled.	**Jag är handikappad.**
	yahg air hand • ee • kap • ad
I'm deaf.	**Jag är döv.**
	yahg air durv

I'm visually/hearing impaired.	**Jag är synskadad/hörselskadad.**
	yahg air <u>sewn</u> • skah • dad/ <u>hur</u> • sel • <u>skah</u> • dad
I'm unable to walk far/use the stairs.	**Jag kan inte gå långt/gå i trappor.**
	yahg kan <u>ihn</u> • ter goa loangt/goa ee <u>trap</u> • ohr
Can I bring my wheelchair?	**Kan jag ta med min rullstol?**
	kan yahg tah meed mihn <u>ruhl</u> • stoal
Are guide dogs permitted?	**Är det tillåtet med ledarhund?**
	air dee tihl • <u>loa</u> • teht meed <u>leed</u> • ar • huhnd
Can you help me?	**Kan du hjälpa mig?**
	kan deu yehl • pa may
Could you open/hold the door?	**Kan du öppna/hålla upp dörren?**
	kan deu <u>urp</u> • na/<u>hoa</u> • la uhp <u>dur</u> • rehn

For Health, see page 144.

FOOD & DRINK

EATING OUT

NEED TO KNOW

Can you recommend a good restaurant/ bar?	**Kan du rekommendera en bra restaurang/pub?** *kan deu reh • koh • mehn • dee • ra ehn brah rehs • teu • <u>rang</u>/peub*
Is there a traditional Swedish/an inexpensive restaurant nearby?	**Finns det något värdshus/någon billigare restaurang i närheten?** *fihns dee <u>noa</u> • goht <u>vairds</u> • heus/ <u>noa</u> • gohn bihl • ih • ga • rer rehs • teu • <u>rang</u> ee <u>nair</u> • <u>hee</u> • tehn*
A table for..., please.	**Ett bord för..., tack.** *eht bohrd furr...tak*
Could we sit...?	**Får vi sitta...?** *foar vee <u>siht</u> • a...*
here/there	**här/där** *hair/dair*
outside	**ute** *<u>eu</u> • ter*

in a non-smoking area	**vid bord för icke-rökare**
	veed bohrd furr
	ee • keh • rur • ka • rer
I'm waiting for someone.	**Jag väntar på någon.**
	yahg vairn • tar poa noa • gohn
Where are the toilets?	**Var finns toaletten?**
	vahr fihns toa • ah • leh • tehn
A menu, please.	**En meny, tack.**
	ehn meh • neu tak
What do you recommend?	**Vad rekommenderar du?**
	vahd reh • koh • mehn • dee • rar deu
I'd like...	**Jag skulle vilja ha...**
	yahg skuh • ler vihl • ya hah...
Some more..., please.	**Lite mer..., tack.**
	lee • ter meer...tak
Enjoy your meal.	**Smaklig måltid.**
	smahk • lihg moal • teed
The check [bill], please.	**Kan jag få räkningen, tack.**
	kan yahg foa rairk • nihng • ehn tak
Is service included?	**Är serveringsavgiften inräknad?**
	air ser • veeh • rihngs • afv • yihf • tehn
	ihn • rairk • nad
Can I pay by credit card?	**Kan jag betala med kreditkort?**
	kan yahg beh • tah • la meed
	kreh • deet • koart
Can I have the receipt, please?	**Kan jag få kvittot, tack?**
	kan yahg foa kvih • toht tak
Thank you.	**Tack.**
	tak

WHERE TO EAT

Can you recommend...?	**Kan du rekommendera...?**
	kan deu reh • koh • mehn • dee • ra...
a restaurant	**en restaurang**
	ehn rehs • teu • rang
a bar	**en bar**
	ehn bahr
a cafe	**ett kafé**
	eht ka • feh
a fast-food place	**en grillbar**
	ehn grihl • bahr
a steakhouse	**ett stekhus**
	eht steek • heus
a cheap restaurant	**en billig restaurang**
	en bihl • eeg reh • stah • eu • rahng
an expensive restaurant	**en dyr restaurang**
	ehn dewr reh • stah • eu • rahng

ⓘ

When it comes to eating out, there are many options, ranging from fast-food stands to five-star restaurants. If you are looking for a quick bite to eat, then a **gatukök** (fast-food stand) is an easy choice. If you are looking for more traditional cuisine, this can be found at a **värdshus** (roadside restaurant), **kafé** (cafe) or **restaurang** (restaurant).

RESERVATIONS & PREFERENCES

I'd like to reserve a table...	**Jag skulle vilja boka ett bord...**
	yahg <u>skuh</u> • ler <u>vihl</u> • ya <u>boh</u> • ka eht bohrd...
for two	**för två**
	furr tvoa
for this evening	**till ikväll**
	tihl ee • <u>kvehl</u>
for tomorrow at...	**imorgon klockan...**
	ee • <u>mo</u> • ron <u>kloh</u> • kan...
A table for two, please.	**Kan jag få ett bord för två tack.**
	kan yahg foa eht bohrd furr tvoa tak
We have a reservation.	**Vi har bokat ett bord.**
	vee hahr <u>boa</u> • kat eht bohrd
My name is...	**Jag heter...**
	yahg <u>hee</u> • tehr...
Could we sit...?	**Får vi sitta...?**
	foar vee <u>siht</u> • a...
here/there	**här/där**
	hair/dair
outside	**ute**
	<u>eu</u> • ter
in a non-smoking	**vid bord för icke-rökare**
	veed bohrd furr
area	*<u>ee</u> • keh • <u>rur</u> • kah • rer*
by the window	**vid fönstret**
	veed <u>furns</u> • treht
in the shade	**i skuggan**
	ee <u>skuh</u> • gan
in the sun	**i solen**
	ee <u>sohl</u> • ehn
Where are the restrooms [toilets]?	**Var finns toaletten?**
	vahr fihns toa • ah • <u>leh</u> • tehn

YOU MAY HEAR...

Har ni bokat?	Do you have a
hahr nee <u>boh</u> • kat	reservation?
Hur många blir ni?	How many?
heur <u>moang</u> • a bleer nee	
Rökare eller icke-rökare?	Smoking or
<u>rur</u> • ka • rer ehl • ehr <u>ee</u> • keh <u>rur</u> • ka • rer	non-smoking?
Vill ni beställa?	Are you ready
vihl nee beh • <u>steh</u> • la	to order?
Vad vill ni beställa?	What would
vahd vihl nee beh • <u>steh</u> • la	you like?
Jag kan rekommendera...	I recommend...
yahg kan reh • koh • mehn • <u>dee</u> • ra...	
Smaklig måltid.	Enjoy your
<u>smahk</u> • lihg <u>moal</u> • teed	meal.

HOW TO ORDER

Excuse me!	**Ursäkta!**
	<u>eur</u> • shehk • ta
We're ready to order.	**Vi vill gärna beställa.**
	vee vihl <u>yair</u> • na beh • <u>steh</u> • la
May I see the	**Kan jag få se vinlistan?**
	kan yahg f<u>oa</u> see
wine list?	<u>veen</u> • lihs • tan
I'd like...	**Jag skulle vilja ha...**
	yahg <u>skuh</u> • ler <u>vihl</u> • ya hah...
a bottle of...	**en flaska...**
	ehn <u>flahs</u> • ka...
a glass of...	**ett glas...**
	eht glahs...

a carafe of...	**en karaff...**
	ehn kah • raf...
The menu, please.	**En meny, tack.**
	ehn meh • neu tak
Do you have...?	**Har ni...?**
	hahr nee...
a menu in English	**en meny på engelska**
	ehn meh • neu poa ehng • ehl • ska
a fixed price menu	**en meny med fast pris**
	ehn meh • neu meed fast prees
a children's menu	**en barnmeny**
	ehn bahrn • meh • neu
What do you recommend?	**Vad rekommenderar ni?**
	vahd reh • koh • mehn • dee • rar nee
What's this?	**Vad är det här?**
	vahd air dee hair
What's in it?	**Vad är det i den?**
	vahd air dee ee dehn
Is it spicy?	**Är den kryddstark?**
	air dehn kreyd • stark
I'd like...	**Jag skulle vilja ha...**
	yahg skuh • ler vihl • ya hah...
More..., please.	**Lite mer..., tack.**
	lee • teh meer...tak
With/Without...	**Med/Utan...**
	meed/eu • tan...
I can't have...	**Jag kan inte äta mat som innehåller...**
	yahg kan ihn • ter air • ta maht som ih • neh • hoal • lehr...
rare	**blodig**
	bloa • dihg
medium	**medium**
	mee • dee • uhm
well done	**genomstekt**
	ye • nom • steekt

It's to go [take away]. **Jag ska ta den med mig.**

yahg skah tah dehn meed may

For Drinks, see page 200.

YOU MAY SEE...

KUVERTAVGIFT	cover charge
FAST PRIS	fixed-price
MENY	menu
DAGENS MENY	menu of the day
DRICKS (INTE) INRÄKNAD	service (not) included
SPECIALITETER	specials

COOKING METHODS

baked	**bakad**
	bah • kad
boiled	**kokt**
	koakt
braised	**bräserad**
	braeh • seeh • rad
breaded	**panerad**
	pah • neeh • rad
creamed	**rörd**
	rurd
diced	**i bitar**
	ee bee • tar
filleted	**filead**
	fih • leeh • ad
fried	**stekt**
	steekt

grilled	**grillad**
	grihl • ad
poached	**pocherad**
	poa • _sheeh_ • rad
roasted	**ugnstekt**
	eungn • steekt
sautéed	**stekt**
	steekt
smoked	**rökt**
	_rur_kt
steamed	**ångkokt**
	oang • koakt
stewed	**stuvad**
	steu • vad
stuffed	**fylld**
	fewld

DIETARY REQUIREMENTS

I am...	**Jag är...**
	yahg air...
diabetic	**diabetiker**
	dee • a • _beh_ • tih • ker
lactose intolerant	**laktosintolerant**
	lak • _toas_ • in • toh • leh • _rant_
vegetarian	**vegetarian**
	veh • geh • ta • ree • _ahn_
vegan	**vegan**
	veh • gahn
I'm allergic to...	**Jag är allergisk mot...**
	yahg air a • _lehr_ • _gihsk_ moat...
I can't eat food that contains...	**Jag kan inte äta mat som innehåller...**
	yahg kan _ihn_ • ter _air_ • ta maht som _ihn_ • neh • hoa • lehr...

dairy	**mejeriprodukter**
	may • eh • <u>ree</u> • proh • duhk • tehr
gluten	**gluten**
	<u>glue</u> • tehn
nut	**nöt**
	n<u>ur</u>t
pork	**fläskkött**
	<u>flehsk</u> • churt
shellfish	**skaldjur**
	<u>skahl</u> • y<u>eu</u>r
spicy food	**kryddad mat**
	<u>krew</u> • dad maht
wheat	**vete**
	<u>veeh</u> • te
Is it halal/kosher?	**Är det halal/kosher?**
	air deht ha • lal/kosh • ehr
Do you have...?	**Har ni...?**
	hahr nee
skimmed milk	**lättmjölk**
	leht • myulk
whole milk	**standardmjölk**
	stahn • dardh • myulk
soya milk	**sojamjölk**
	soh • ya • myulk

DINING WITH CHILDREN

Do you have a children's menu?	**Har ni en barnmeny?**
	hahr nee ehn <u>bahrn</u> • meh • neu
Can you bring a high chair, please?	**Kan jag få en barnstol, tack?**
	kan yahg foa ehn <u>bahrn</u> • st<u>oa</u>l tak
Where can I feed/ change the baby?	**Var kan jag mata/byta på babyn?**
	vahr kan yahg <u>mah</u> • ta/<u>bew</u> • ta poa <u>bai</u> • been

| Can you warm this? | **Kan ni värma det här?** |
| | *kan nee <u>vair</u> • ma dee hair* |

For Traveling with Children, see page 134.

HOW TO COMPLAIN

How much longer will our food be?	**Hur länge till behöver vi vänta?**
	heur <u>lehng</u> • er tihl beh • <u>hur</u> • ver vee <u>vehn</u> • ta
We can't wait any longer.	**Vi kan inte vänta längre.**
	vee kan <u>ihn</u> • ter <u>vehn</u> • ta <u>lehng</u> • rer
We're leaving.	**Vi går nu.**
	vee goar neu
That's not what I ordered.	**Det här har jag inte beställt.**
	dee hair hahr yahg <u>ihn</u> • ter beh • <u>stehlt</u>
I asked for...	**Jag beställde...**
	yahg beh • <u>stehl</u> • der...
I can't eat this.	**Jag kan inte äta det här.**
	yahg kan <u>ihn</u> • ter <u>air</u> • ta dee hair
This is too...	**Det här är för...**
	dee hair air furr...
cold/hot	**kallt/varmt**
	kalt/varmt
salty/spicy	**salt/kryddat**
	salt/<u>krew</u> • dat
tough/bland	**segt/smaklöst**
	sekt<u>/smahk</u> • lurst
This isn't clean/ fresh.	**Det här är inte rent/färskt.**
	dee hair air <u>ihn</u> • ter reent/fairskt

PAYING

| The check [bill], please. | **Kan jag få räkningen, tack.** |
| | *kan yahg foa <u>rairk</u> • nihng • ehn tak* |

We'd like to pay separately.	**Vi vill betala var för sig.** *vee vihl beh • tah • la vahr furr say*
It's all together.	**Allt tillsammans.** *alt tihl • saa • mans*
Is service included?	**Är serveringsavgiften inräknad?** *air sehr • veeh • rihngs • afv • yihf • ten ihn • rairk • nad*
What's this amount for?	**Vad står den här summan för?** *vahd stoar dehn hair suhm • an furr*
I didn't have that. I had…	**Jag åt inte det. Jag åt…** *yahg oat ihn • ter dee yahg oat…*
Can I pay by credit card?	**Kan jag betala med kreditkort?** *kan yahg beh • tah • la meed kreh • deet • koart*
Can I have an itemized bill/ a receipt?	**Kan jag få en specificerad räkning/ett kvitto?** *kan yahg foa ehn speh • seh • fee • ee • rad rairk • nihng/eht kvih • toh*
That was a very good meal.	**Det var en mycket god måltid.** *dee vahr ehn mew • ker goad moal • teed*
I've already paid.	**Jag har redan betalat.** *yahg hahr reh • dan beh • tah • lat*

MEALS & COOKING

BREAKFAST

apelsin *a • pehl • seen*	orange
bacon *bay • kohn*	bacon

bröd
brurd — bread

filmjölk
feel • myurlk — thick yogurt

frukostflingor
fruh • kohst • flihng • or — (cold) cereal

fruktjuice
fruhkt • yoas — fruit juice

grapefrukt
grape • fruhkt — grapefruit

gröt
grurt — (hot) cereal

havregryn
hafv • reh • greun — oatmeal

honung
hoa • neung — honey

kaffe...
ka • fer... — coffee...

  med mjölk
  meed myurlk — with milk

  med socker
  meed soh • ker — with sugar

  med sötningsmedel
  meed surt • nihngs • mee • dehl — with artificial sweetener

  utan koffein
  eu • tan koh • feen — decaf

kallskuret
kal • skeu • reht — cold cuts [charcuterie]

kokt ägg
koakt ehg — boiled egg

korv
kohrv — sausage

marmelad
mar • meh • lahd — marmalade

mjölk
myurlk
milk

muffin
muh • fihn
muffin

müsli
mews • lee
granola [muesli]

omelett
ohm • eh • leht
omelet

ost
oast
cheese

rostat bröd
roahs • tat brurd
toast

småbröd
smoa • brurd
roll

smör
smur
butter

stekt ägg
steekt ehg
fried egg

Frukost (breakfast) is usually served from 7:00 to 10:00 a.m. Hotels and guesthouses offer a large buffet selection of cheese, cold meat, bread, eggs, cereals and **filmjölk** (thick yogurt). **Lunch** (lunch) is served from as early as 11:00 a.m. Although many Swedes have a warm meal at lunchtime, some opt for a sandwich or a salad. This is the best time to try the **dagens rätt** (specialty of the day). **Middag** (dinner) is normally eaten early, around 6:00 or 7:00 p.m., though many restaurants continue serving until late, especially at the weekend. Many Swedes will also eat a meal later in the evening, referred to as **kvällsmål;** this evening meal usually includes sandwiches, yogurt or soup.

sylt *sewlt*	jam
thé *tee*	tea
vatten *va • tehrn*	water
yoghurt *yoh • geurt*	yogurt
ägg *ehg*	egg
äggröra *ehg • rur • ra*	scrambled eggs
äpple *ehp • leh*	apple

APPETIZERS

färska räkor *fair • ska rair • kohr*	unshelled shrimp [prawns], served with toast, butter and mayonnaise
förrätt *furr • reht*	appetizer [starter]
gravlax *grafv • lax*	marinated salmon
löjrom *lurj • rohm*	bleak roe, served with chopped, raw onions and sour cream and eaten on toast
rökt lax *rurkt lax*	smoked salmon
sill *sihl*	marinated herring

sillbricka
sihl • brih • ka
S.O.S. (smör, ost och sill)
ehs oa ehs (smur oast ohk sil)

variety of marinated herring
a small plate of marinated herring, bread, butter and cheese

toast skagen
toast skah • gehn

toast with chopped shrimp [prawns] in mayonnaise, topped with bleak roe

viltpastej
vihlt • pa • stay

game pâté

SOUP

buljong
beul • yong

broth

fisksoppa
fihsk • sop • a

fish soup

grönsakssoppa
grurn • sahks • sohp • a

vegetable soup

kall soppa
kal sohp • a

cold soup

kycklingsoppa
chewk • lihng • sohp • a

chicken soup

kött och grönsakssoppa
churt • oa • grurn • sahk • sohp • a

meat and vegetable soup

köttsoppa
churt • sohp • a

a hearty soup of beef, vegetables and dumplings

löksoppa
lurk • sohp • a

onion soup

nyponsoppa
new • pohn • sohp • a

rose-hip soup

oxsvanssoppa
oax • svans • sohp • a

oxtail soup

potatissoppa
poa • tah • tihs • sohp • a

potato soup

rörd soppa
rurrd sohp • a

cream soup

sparrissoppa
spa • rihs • sohp • a

asparagus soup

spenatsoppa
speh • nat • sohp • a

a rich soup made
from spinach,
potatoes, milk and
cream

tomatsoppa
toa • maht • soh • pa

tomato soup

ärtsoppa
airt • sohp • a

green or yellow pea
soup

FISH & SEAFOOD

abborre
ah • bohr • er

perch

ansjovis
an • shoa • vees

anchovy

blåmussla
bloa • muhs • la

blue mussel

braxen
brak • sehn

sea bream

böckling
burk • lihng

smoked Baltic
herring

fisk
fihsk

fish

forell
foa • rehl

trout

färska räkor
fairs • ka rair • kohr

unshelled shrimp
[prawns]

gravlax
grafv • lax

marinated salmon

gädda
yeh • da

sea perch

halstrad fisk
hal • strahd fihsk

grilled fish

halstrad forell med färskpotatis
_hal • strad foa • rehl med
fairsk • poa • tah • tihs_

grilled trout with
new potatoes

havsabborre
hafs • a • boh • rer

sea bass

hummer
huhm • ehr

lobster

hälleflundra
heh • leh • fleun • dra

halibut

inlagd sill
ihn • lagd sil

marinated (pickled)
herring

Janssons frestelse
yahn • sons frehs • tehl • ser

casserole with
potatoes and
anchovies

kammussla
kam • muhs • la

scallop

kolja
kohl • ya

haddock

krabba
kra • ba

crab

kräfta
krehf • ta

crayfish

kummel
keu • mel

hake

lax
lax

salmon

löjrom
lury • rohm

bleak roe with chopped, raw onions and sour cream; served on toast

makrill
mak • rihl

mackerel

marulk
mahr • eulk

monkfish

matjesill
ma • shcheh • sihl

marinated herring

multe
muhl • ter

mullet

mussla
muhs • la

mussel

mört
murt

roach (type of fish)

ostron
oas • tron

oyster

piggvar
pihg • vahr

turbot

rimmad lax med stuvad potatis
rihm • ahd lax meed
steu • vad poa • tah • tihs

lightly salted salmon with creamed potatoes and dill

rocka
roh • ka

ray (type of fish)

räkor
rair • kohr

shrimp [prawns]

röding
rur • dihng

char

rödspätta
rurd • speh • ta

plaice

rökt fisk
rurkt fisk

smoked fish

rökt lax
rurkt lax

smoked salmon

rökt ål
rurkt oal

smoked eel

sardin
sar • deen

sardine

sill
sihl

herring

sillbricka
sihl • brih • ka

variety of
marinated herring

sillsallad
sihl • sal • ad

beet and herring
salad

sjötunga
sjur • tuhng • a

sole

skaldjur
skahl • yeur

shellfish

skaldjurssallad
skahl • yeurs • sal • ad

shellfish salad

skarpsill
skarp • sihl

herring

småsill
smoa • sihl

herring

S.O.S. (smör, ost och sill)
ehs oa ehs (smur oast ohk sihl)

small plate of
marinated herring,
bread, butter and
cheese

stekt fisk
steekt fisk

fried fish

strömming
struhrm • ihng

sprats (small Baltic
herring) filleted
and sandwiched in
pairs with dill and
butter in the middle

strömmingsflundra _strurm_ • ihngs • fleun • dra	Baltic herring, filleted and sandwiched in pairs, fried, with dill and butter filling
stuvad abborre _steu_ • vad _a_ • boh • rer	perch poached with onion, parsley and lemon
tonfisk _toan_ • fihsk	tuna
torsk tohrshk	cod
ugnsbakad fisk _eungns_ • bah • kad fihsk	oven-baked fish
vitling _veet_ • lihng	whiting
västkustsallad _vehst_ • kuhst • _sal_ • ad	west coast salad, with shrimp [prawns] and mussels
ål oal	eel
ångkokt fisk _oang_ • koakt fisk	steamed fish

MEAT & POULTRY

anka _ang_ • ka	duck
bacon _bay_ • kon	bacon
biffkött _bihf_ • churt	beef
biffstek _bihf_ • steek	steak

bog
boag
shoulder (cut of meat)

broiler
broy • lehr
spring chicken

entrecote
an • treh • koat
sirloin steak

falukorv
fah • leu • kohrv
lightly spiced sausage

fasan
fa • sahn
pheasant

filé
fih • leh
filet mignon

fläsk
flehsk
pork

fläskben
flehsk • been
ham bone

fläskfilé
flehsk • fih • leh
fillet of pork

fläskkarré
flehsk • ka • reh
pork loin

fläskkorv
flehsk • kohrv
spicy, boiled pork sausage

fläsklägg
flehsk • lehg
knuckle of pork

fågel
foa • gehl
poultry

får
foar
mutton

get
yeet
kid (goat)

grillad kyckling
grihl • ahd chewk • lihng
grilled chicken

gås
goas
goose

hamburgare
ham • beur • ya • rer

hamburger

hare
hah • rer

rabbit

hjort
yohrt

deer

isterband
ihs • tehr • band

sausage of pork,
barley and beef

kalkon
kal • koan

turkey

kallskuret
kal • skeu • reht

cold cuts
 [charcuterie]

kalops
ka • lohps

beef stew

kalvkött
kalv • churt

veal

kalvsylta
kalv • sewl • ta

cold veal in jelly

karré
ka • reh

tenderloin

kokt skinka
koakt shihng • ka

boiled ham

korv
kohrv

sausage

kotlett
koht • lehtt

cutlet

kyckling
chewk • lihng

chicken

kycklingbröst
chewk • lihng • brurst

chicken breast

kycklinglever
chewk • lihng • lee • vehr

chicken liver

kåldomar med gräddsås och lingon
koal • dohl • mar meed grehd • soas ohk

chopped [minced]
meat and rice

lihng • ohn	stuffed in cabbage leaves
kött	meat
churt	
köttbulle	meatball
churt • buh • ler	
köttfärs	chopped [minced]
churt • fairs	beef
lamm	lamb
lamm	
lammgryta	lamb stew
lamm • grew • ta	
lever	liver
lee • vehr	
leverpastej	liver pâté
lee • vehr pa • stay	
lägg	shank (top of leg)
lehg	
lövbiff	fried, thinly sliced
lurv • bihf	beef, with onions
medaljong	small fillet of cut
meh • dal • yong	meat
njure	kidney
nyeu • rer	
nötkött	red meat
nurt • churt	
oxkött	ox
oax • churt	
oxrullad	braised roll of beef
oax • reu • lahd	
oxsvans	oxtail
oax • svans	
pannbiff	beef patty
pan • bihf	

prinskorv
prihns • kohrv

small pork sausage

pärlhöns
pairl • hurns

guinea fowl

ragu
ra • guh

beef stew

rapphöna
rap • hurna

partridge

ren
reen

reindeer

renstek med svampsås
reen • steek meed svamp • soas

roast reindeer with mushroom sauce

revbensspjäll
reev • beens • spehl

spareribs

rostbiff
rohst • bihf

roast beef

rumpstek
ruhmp • steek

rump steak

rådjur
roa • yeur

venison

rådjursstek
roa • yeur • steek

roast of venison

rökt renstek
rurkt reen • steek

smoked reindeer

rökt skinka
rurkt shihng • ka

smoked ham

sadel
sah • dehl

saddle (cut of meat)

salamikorv
sa • lah • mee • kohrv

salami

schnitzel
shniht • sehl

escallope

sillsallad
sihl • sal • ad

beet and herring salad

sjömansbiff
_sh**ur** • mans • _bihf__

casserole of fried beef, onions and potatoes, braised in beer

skinka
shihng • ka

ham

spädgris
spaird • grees

an unweaned piglet

stekt kyckling
steekt _chewk • lihng_

fried chicken (not breaded)

T-benstek
tee • been • steek

T-bone steak

tunga
tuhng • a

tongue (cow)

(i)

If you've never heard of typical Swedish food, you may at least be familiar with the famous **smörgåsbord** — it is a buffet meal on a grand scale, presented on a large, beautifully decorated table. You start at one end of the table, usually the one with the cold seafood dishes, marinated herring, **Janssons frestelse** (literally, Jansson's temptation, a potato and anchovies casserole) and salad. Then you work your way through the cold meat, meatballs, sausage, omelets and vegetables. Finally, you end at the cheeseboard and desserts. You're welcome to start all over again; the price is set, and you can eat as much as you like. You will find that the Swedes tend to drink **akvavit** (aquavit) or beer with the feast, although an accompanying glass of wine is becoming more common for those who find **akvavit** too strong.

At Christmas time, the **smörgåsbord** becomes a **julbord** (Christmas buffet), popular in homes and restaurants alike.

ugnsstekt kyckling	roast chicken
eungn • steekt chewk • lihng	
vaktel	quail
vak • tehl	
varmkorv	hot dog
varm • kohrv	
wienerschnitzel	breaded veal cutlet
vee • nehr • shniht • sehl	
vildand	wild duck
vihld • and	
vilt	game
vihlt	
älg	moose
ehly	
älgfilé	fillet of moose
ehly • fih • leh	
älgstek	moose roast
ehly • steek	
älgstek med svampsås	roast moose with
ehly • steek meed svamp • soas	mushroom sauce

VEGETABLES & STAPLES

avokado	avocado
a • voh • kah • doa	
basilika	basil
ba • sih • lee • ka	
blandsallad	mixed salad
bland • sal • ad	
blomkål	cauliflower
bloam • koal	
bouquet garni	mixed herbs
boh • keh gar • nee	
böna...	...bean
bur • na...	

bond
boand
broad

bryt
brewt
kidney

grön
grurn
green

vax
vax
butter

broccoli
broh • koh • lee
broccoli

brysselkål
brew • sehl • koal
Brussel sprout

bröd
brurd
bread

bönskott
burn • skoht
bean sprout

champinjon
sham • pihn • yoan
mushroom

chilipeppar
shee • lih • peh • par
chili pepper

dragon
dra • goan
tarragon

endiv
an • deev
endive

fullkornsmjöl
fuhl • kohrns • myurl
whole wheat flour

fänkål
fehn • koal
fennel

färskpotatis
fairsk • poa • tah • this
new potato

gräslök
grairs • lurk
chive

grön paprika
grurn pah • pree • ka
green pepper

grönsak *grurn • sahk*	vegetable
grönsallad *grurn • sal • ad*	lettuce
gurka *geur • ka*	cucumber
haricots verts *ar • ee • koh • vair*	green bean
honung *hoa • neung*	honey
ingefära *ih • ng • eh • fai • ra*	ginger
kanel *ka • neel*	cinnamon
kantarell *kan • ta • rehl*	chanterelle mushroom
kapris *ka • prees*	caper
kikärta *cheek • air • ta*	chickpea
kokt potatis *koakt poa • tah • tihs*	boiled potato
kronärtskocka *kroan • airts • koh • ka*	artichoke
kryddpeppar *krewd • peh • par*	allspice
kummin *keu • meen*	caraway
kål *koal*	cabbage
kålrot *koal • roht*	turnip
källkrasse *chehl • kra • ser*	watercress

körvel
chur • vehl
chervil

lagerblad
lah • gehr • blahd
bay leaf

lins
lihns
lentil

lök
lurk
onion

majs
mays
sweet corn

mjöl
myurl
flour

morot
moa • roht
carrot

muskot
muhs • koht
nutmeg

mynta
mewn • ta
mint (herb)

nejlika
nay • lih • ka
clove

nudel
neu • dehl
noodle

olja och vinäger
oal • ya ohk vee • nai • gehr
oil and vinegar

palsternacka
pal • stehr • na • ka
parsnip

paprika
pah • prih • ka
pepper (fresh)

pasta
pas • ta
pasta

persilja
pair • shihl • ya
parsley

potatis
poa • tah • tihs
potato

potatissallad
poa • <u>tah</u> • tihs • <u>sal</u> • ad

potato salad

pumpa
<u>puhm</u> • pa

pumpkin

purjolök
<u>peur</u> • yoh • lurk

leek

ris
rees

rice

rosmarin
roas • ma • <u>reen</u>

rosemary

rova
<u>roa</u> • va

turnip

rädisa
<u>raid</u> • dih • sa

radish

röd paprika
rurd <u>pah</u> • pree • ka

sweet red pepper

rödbeta
<u>rurd</u> • bee • ta

beet

rödkål
<u>rurd</u> • koal

red cabbage

salladshuvud
<u>sal</u> • ads • heu • vuhd

head of lettuce

saltgurka
<u>salt</u> • geur • ka

salted, pickled
gherkin

salvia
sal • <u>vee</u> • a

sage

schalottenlök
sha • <u>loh</u> • tehn • <u>lurk</u>

shallot [spring
onion]

selleri
seh • leh • <u>ree</u>

celery

sirap
<u>seh</u> • rap

syrup

skogssvamp
<u>skoags</u> • svamp

field mushroom

smör
smurr
butter

sockerärta
soh • kehr • air • ta
sugar snap pea
[mangetout]

sparris
spar • ihs
asparagus

spenat
speh • naht
spinach

squash
skoawsh
squash (vegetable)

svamp
svamp
mushroom

sötpotatis
surt • poa • tah • tihs
sweet potato

timjan
tihm • yan
thyme

tomat
toa • maht
tomato

tomater och lök
toa • mah • ter ohk lurk
tomato and onion
salad

vanilj
va • nihly
vanilla

vattenkrasse
kra • ser
watercress

vetemjöl
vee • teh • mjurl
wheat flour
(regular)

vild champinjon
vihl • da sham • pihn • yoan
wild mushroom

vitkål
veet • koal
white cabbage

vitlök
veet • lurk
garlic

vårlök
voar • lurk
shallot [spring
onion]

zucchini
seu • kee • nee

zucchini [courgette]

äggplanta
ehg • plan • ta

eggplant
[aubergine]

ärta
air • ta

peas

ättiksgurka
eh • tiks • geur • kah

pickled gherkin

FRUIT

ananas
an • a • nas

pineapple

apelsin
a • pehl • seen

orange

aprikos
a • prih • koas

apricot

banan
ba • nahn

banana

bigarrå
bih • ga • roa

sweet morello
cherry

björnbär
byurn • bair

blackberry

blå vindruva
bloa veen • dreu • va

black grape

blåbär
bloa • bair

blueberry

citron
see • troan

lemon

dadel
dahd • ehl

date

enbär
een • bair

juniper berry

fikon
fee • kohn

fig

frukt *fruhkt*	fruit
grapefrukt *grape • fruhkt*	grapefruit
grön vindruva *grurn veen • dreu • va*	green grape
hallon *hal • ohn*	raspberry
hasselnöt *ha • sehl • nurt*	hazelnut
hjortron *yoahr • tron*	cloudberry
jordgubbe *yoard • guh • ber*	strawberry
jordnöt *yoard • nurt*	peanut
katrinplommon *ka • treen • ploa • mohn*	prune
kiwifrukt *kee • vee • fruhkt*	kiwi
kokosnöt *koa • kos • nurt*	coconut
krusbär *kreus • bair*	gooseberry
körsbär *churs • bair*	cherry
lingon *lihng • ohn*	lingonberry
mandarin *man • da • reen*	tangerine/ mandarin orange
mandel *man • dehl*	almond
(vatten)melon *(va • tehrn)meh • loan*	(water)melon

mullbär
muhl • bair

mulberry

nektarin
nehk • ta • reen

nectarine

oliv
o • leev

olive

persika
pairsh • ih • ka

peach

plommon
plohm • on

plum

pomegranat äpple
pom • eh • gra • naht • ehp • leh

pomegranate

päron
pai • rohn

pear

rabarber
rah • bar • behr

rhubarb

russin
ruh • sihn

raisin

röd vinbär
rurd veen • bair

red currant

smultron
smeul • trohn

wild strawberry

sultana
suhl • tahn • a

sultana raisin

svart vinbär
svart veen • bair

black currant

valnöt
vahl • nurt

walnut

vinbär
veen • bair

currant

vindruva
veen • dreu • va

grape

äpple
ehp • leh

apple

CHEESE

fårost
foar • oast
ewe's milk cheese

getost
yeet • oast
goat cheese

grevé
greh • vee
a semi-hard
cheese similar to
gouda and
emmentaler

herrgårdsost
hehr • goards • oast
a semi-hard
cheese with
large holes and a
nutty flavor

kryddost
krewd • oast
a sharp, strong
cheese with
caraway seeds

mesost
mees • oast
a soft, sweet,
yellowish whey
cheese

mjukost
myeuk • oast
soft cheese

ost
oast
cheese

ostbricka
oast • brih • ka
cheese plate

prästost
prehst • oast
hard cheese with a
strong, rich flavor

svecia
sveh • see • a
semi-hard cheeses

västerbotten
vehs • tehr • boh • tehrn
a sharp, tangy, hard
and very strong
cheese from the
north of Sweden

ädelost
air • dehl • oast

a blue cheese with a sharp taste, similar to Roquefort

DESSERT

efterrätt
ehf • tehr • reht

dessert

friterad camembert med hjortronsylt
free • _tee_ • rad cam • ehm • _behrt_ meed _yoh_ • tron • sewlt

deep-fried camembert with cloudberry jam

fruktsallad
fruhkt • sal • ad

fruit salad

glass
glas

ice cream

jordgubbar med grädde
yoard • guhb • ar meed _greh_ • deh

strawberries and cream

kaka
kah • ka

cake

mandeltårta
man • dehl • toar • ta

almond tart

marängsviss
mah • _rehng_ • svis

meringue with whipped cream and chocolate sauce

mjuk pepparkaka
myeuk _peh_ • par • kah • ka

soft ginger cake

ostkaka
oast • kah • ka

traditional southern Sweden curd cake

tårta
toarta

sponge-based fruit or cream cake

våffla (med sylt och grädde)
vohf • la meed sewlt ohk _greh_ • der

waffle (with jam and whipped cream)

äppelpaj
_eh_ • pehl • _pay_

apple tart

äppelkaka
eh • pehl • kah • ka

apple cake

äppelring
ehp • ehl • rihng

apple fritter

SAUCES & CONDIMENTS

peppar
peh • par

pepper

salt
salt

salt

senap
see • nap

mustard

socker
soh • kehr

sugar

sötningsmedel
surt • nihngs • mee • dehl

artificial sweetener

ketchup
keht • shuhp

ketchup

AT THE MARKET

Where are the carts [trolleys]/baskets?	**Var finns shoppingvagnarna/ shoppingkorgarna?** *vahr fihns shoh • pihng • vagn • nar • na/ shoh • pihng • kohr • yar • na*
Where is/are...?	**Var finns...?** *vahr fihns...*
I'd like some of this/that.	**Jag skulle vilja ha lite av det här/ det där.** *yahg skuh • ler vihl • ya hah lee • teh afv dee hair/dee dair*
Can I taste it?	**Får jag smaka?** *foar yahg smah • ka*
I'd like...	**Jag skulle vilja ha...** *yahg skuh • ler vihl • ya hah...*

a kilo/half-kilo of…	**ett kilo/halvt kilo…**
	eht <u>chee</u> • loh/halft <u>chee</u> • loh…
a liter/half-liter of…	**en liter/halv liter…**
	ehn <u>lee</u> • ter/halv <u>lee</u> • ter…
a piece of…	**en bit av…**
	ehn beet afv…
a slice of…	**en skiva av…**
	ehn <u>shee</u> • va afv…
More/Less than that.	**Mer/Mindre än det där.**
	meer/<u>mihn</u> • dreh ehn dee dair
How much does it cost?	**Hur mycket kostar det?**
	heur <u>mew</u> • ker <u>kos</u> • tar dee
Where do I pay?	**Var kan jag betala?**
	vahr kan yahg beh • <u>tah</u> • la
Can I have a bag?	**Kan jag få en påse?**
	kan yahg foa ehn <u>poa</u> • seh
I'm being helped.	**Tack, jag har fått hjälp.**
	tak yahg hahr foat yehlp

YOU MAY HEAR…

Kan jag hjälpa er?
kan yahg <u>yehl</u> • pa eer

Can I help you?

Vad vill ni beställa?
vahd vihl nee beh • <u>steh</u> • la

What would you like?

Något annat?
<u>noa</u> • goht <u>an</u> • nat

Anything else?

Det kostar…kronor.
dee <u>kos</u> • tar…<u>kroa</u> • nohr

That's…kronor.

(i)

Measurements in Europe are metric — and that applies to the weight of food too. If you tend to think in pounds and ounces, it's worth brushing up on what the equivalent is before you go shopping for fruit and veg in markets and supermarkets. Five hundred grams, or half a kilo, is a common quantity to order, and that converts to just over a pound (17.65 ounces, to be precise).

(i)

Although Sweden still has many small, specialty shops, they are slowly giving way to **köpcentrum** (shopping centers), especially in larger towns. You can still find markets that sell fresh fruit and vegetables as well as flowers and some handicrafts. **Julmarknaden** (the traditional Christmas market) in Stockholm is reminiscent of times gone by. Supermarkets can be found in most large towns, cities and suburbs. **Närbutiker** (corner shops), as well as **Pressbyrån** (newsstand chain) sell a good range of food. In Stockholm, **Östermalmshallen** and **Hötorgshallen** (market halls) sell fresh meat — including reindeer and moose — fish and poultry. Swedes enjoy a variety of fish and seafood, and one will find a good selection in most restaurants and supermarkets. If you visit Sweden in August, you will no doubt enjoy a **kräftkalas** (crayfish party). There is not much meat on a crayfish, but when helped down with a few glasses of **akvavit** (aquavit) and some salad and cheese, it makes for an unforgettable evening.

IN THE KITCHEN

bottle opener	**flasköppnare**	
	flask • eup • na • rehr	
bowl	**djup tallrik**	
	y**eup** _tal_ • rihk	
can opener	**konservöppnare**	
	kohn • _sehrv_ • urp • nah • rer	
corkscrew	**korkskruv**	
	kohrk • skr**euv**	
cup	**kopp**	
	kohp	
fork	**gaffel**	
	gahf • ehl	
frying pan	**stekpanna**	
	steek • pan • na	
glass	**glas**	
	glahs	
knife	**kniv**	
	kneev	
measuring cup/	**mått/måttsked**	
spoon	moat/_moat_ • sheed	
napkin	**servett**	
	sehr • _vehtt_	
plate	**tallrik**	
	tal • rihk	
pot	**gryta**	
	grew • ta	
saucepan	**kastrull**	
	kas • _truhl_	
spatula	**steekspade**	
	steek • spah • der	
spoon	**sked**	
	sheed	

DRINKS

NEED TO KNOW

May I see the wine list/drink menu?	**Kan jag få se vinlistan/ drinklistan?** *kan yahg foa see <u>veen</u> • lihs • tan/ <u>drihnk</u> • lihs • tan*
What do you recommend?	**Vad rekommenderar ni?** *vahd reh • koh • mehn • <u>dee</u> • rar nee*
I'd like a bottle/glass of red/white wine.	**Jag skulle vilja ha en flaska/ett glas rött/ vitt vin.** *yahg <u>skuh</u> • ler <u>vihl</u> • ya hah ehn <u>flas</u> • ka/eht glahs ruhrt/viht veen*
The house wine, please.	**Husets vin, tack.** *<u>heu</u> • sehts veen tak*
Another bottle/glass, please.	**En flaska/Ett glas till, tack.** *ehn <u>flas</u> • ka/eht glahs tihl tak*
I'd like a local beer.	**Jag skulle vilja ha en öl från trakten.** *yahg <u>skuh</u> • ler <u>vihl</u> • ya hah ehn **url** fron <u>trak</u> • tehn*
Let me buy you a drink.	**Får jag bjuda på en drink.** *foar yahg <u>byeu</u> • da poa ehn drihnk*
Cheers!	**Skål!** *skoal*
A coffee/tea, please.	**En kopp kaffe/te, tack.** *ehn kohp <u>ka</u> • fer/tee tak*
Black.	**Svart.** *Svart*
With...	**Med...** *meed...*

milk	**mjölk**
	myuhlk
sugar	**socker**
	soh • kehr
artificial sweetener	**sötningsmedel**
	surt • nihngs • mee • dehl
decaf	**utan koffein** *eu • tan koh • feen*
..., please.	**..., tack.**
	...tak
Juice	**Juice**
	yoas
Soda	**sodavatten**
	soa • da • va • tehrn
Sparkling water	**Vatten med kolsyra**
	va • tehrn meed koal • sew • ra
Still water	**Vatten utan kolsyra**
	va • tehrn eu • tan koal • sew • ra
Is the tap water safe to drink?	**Kan man dricka kranvattnet?**
	kan man drih • ka krahn • vat • neht

NON-ALCOHOLIC DRINKS

alkoholfri dryck
al • ko • hoal • free drewk
non-alcoholic drink

ananasjuice
an • a • nas • yoas
pineapple juice

apelsinjuice
a • pehl • seen • yoas
orange juice

cola
koa • la
cola

fruktjuice
fruhkt • yoas
fruit juice

juice
yoas

juice

kaffe
ka • fer

coffee

läsk
lehsk

soft drink

milkshake
milk • shake

milk shake

mineralvatten
mihn • eh • rahl • va • tehrn

mineral water

mjölk
myurlk

milk

saft
saft

squash (fruit cordial)

sockerdricka
soh • kehr • drih • ka

lemonade

sodavatten
soa • da • va • tehrn

soda water

(i)

For afternoon tea (usually enjoyed with lemon) or coffee you can do no better than the typical Swedish **konditori** (patisserie or coffee shop). Help yourself to as many cups as you like while indulging in a slice of **prinsesstårta** (sponge cake with cream and custard, covered with green marzipan), **mazarin** (almond tart, topped with icing) or a **wienerbröd** (Danish pastry). Try **saffransbullar** (saffron buns) and **pepparkakor** (ginger cookies) at Christmas. Most **konditori** are self-service, but some of the more elegant ones and those in hotels provide full service. Coffee is definitely the national drink, and it is always freshly brewed. It is commonly drunk black, but ask for **mjölk** (milk) or **grädde** (cream) if you like it that way.

thé med mjölk/citron *tee meed myurlk/* *see • troan*	tea with milk/ lemon
tomatjuice *toa • maht • yoas*	tomato juice
tonic *toh • nihk*	tonic water
varmchoklad *varm shoa • klahd*	hot chocolate
vatten med/utan kolsyra *va • tehrn meed/ eu • tan koal • sew • ra*	sparkling/ still water

YOU MAY HEAR...

Får jag bjuda på en drink? *foar yahg* *bjeu • da pao ehn drink*	Can I buy you a drink?
Med mjölk/socker? *meed myurlk/soh • ker*	With milk/ sugar?
Vatten med/utan kolsyra? *va • tehrn meed/ eu • tan koal • sew • ra*	Sparkling/Still water?

APERITIFS, COCKTAILS & LIQUEURS

akvavit *a • kva • veet*	aquavit, the famous Swedish grain- or potato- based spirit
cognac *kohn • yak*	brandy
gin *jihn*	gin

glögg
glurg
mulled wine with port and spices, served hot

herrgårdsakvavit
hair • goards • a • kva • veet
aquavit, flavored with caraway seeds and whisky

likör
lih • kurr
liqueur

portvin
port • veen
port

punsch
peunsh
sweet liqueur

rom
rohm
rum

sherry
sheh • ree
sherry

skåne
skoa • ner
aquavit, flavored with aniseed and caraway seeds

sprit
spreet
spirits

vermouth
vehr • meutt
vermouth

vodka...
vod • ka...
vodka...

  med is
  meed ees
on the rocks [with ice]

  med tonic
  meed toh • nihk
with tonic water

  med vatten
  meed va • tehrn
with water

whisky
vihs • kee
whisky

BEER

burköl	canned beer
buhrk • url	
fatöl	draft [draught]
faht • url	
lättöl	light beer
leht • url	
öl på flaska	bottled beer local/
url poa fla • ska	imported
utan alkohol	non-alcoholic
uh • tan al • koh • hohl	

Beer is probably the most popular alcoholic drink
in Sweden, and there are many good Swedish breweries.
Beer with an alcohol content above 3%, called **starköl**,
can only be bought in **Systembolaget** (state liquor store);
lättöl and **folköl**, which are below 3% alcohol content, can
be bought in grocery stores and supermarkets. You will
find many well known international beers, but the most
common are Carlsberg, Heineken and Swedish brews such
as Pripps and Falcon.

WINE

dessertvin	dessert wine
deh • sair • veen	
husets vin	house wine
heu • sehts veen	
mousserande	sparkling
moa • see • ran • der	

rosé
roh • seh

blush [rosé]

rött
ruhrt

red

sött
suhrt

sweet

torrt
tohrt

dry

vitt
viht

white

champagne
shahm • pany

champagne

ON THE MENU

abborre
ah • bohr • er

perch

akvavit
a • kva • veet

aquavit, the famous Swedish grain- or potato-based spirit

alkoholfri dryck
al • ko • hoal • free drewk

non-alcoholic drink

ananas
an • a • nas

pineapple

ananasjuice
an • a • nas • yoas

pineapple juice

anka
ang • ka

duck

ansjovis
an • shoa • vees

anchovy

apelsin
a • pehl • seen

orange

apelsinjuice *a • pehl • <u>seen</u> • yoas*	orange juice
aprikos *a • prih • <u>koa</u>s*	apricot
avokado *a • voh • <u>kah</u> • doa*	avocado
bacon *<u>bay</u> • kon*	bacon
bakelse *<u>bah</u> • kehl • sehr*	piece of cake
bakverk *<u>bahk</u> • verk*	pastry
banan *ba • <u>nahn</u>*	banana
basilika *ba • sih • <u>lee</u> • ka*	basil
biffkött *<u>bihf</u> • churt*	beef
biffstek *<u>bif</u> • steek*	steak
bigarrå *bih • ga • <u>roa</u>*	sweet morello cherry
bit *beet*	slice

björnbär
byurn • bair
blackberry

blandade
blan • da • der
assorted

blandade grönsaker
blan • da • der
grurn • sah • kehr
mixed vegetables

blandade kryddor
blan • da • der krew • dohr
mixed herbs

blandade nötter
blan • da • der nur • tehr
assorted nuts

blandsallad
bland • sal • ad
mixed salad

blodig
bloa • dihg
rare

blomkål
bloam • koal
cauliflower

blå vindruva
bloa veen • dreu • va
black grape

blåbär
bloa • bair
blueberry

blåbärssylt
bloa • bairs • sewlt
blueberry jam

blåmussla
bloa • muhs • la
blue mussel

bog
boag
shoulder (cut of meat)

bondböna
boand • bur • nohr
broad bean

bordsvin
boards • veen
table wine

bouquet garni
boh • keh gar • nee
mixed herbs

braxen
brak • sehn
sea bream

broccoli
broh • loh • lee

broccoli

broiler
broy • lehr

spring chicken

brylépudding
brew • _lee_ • peu • dihng

crème brulee

brysselkål
brew • sehl • _koal_

brussel sprout

brytböna
brewt • bur • na

kidney bean

brännvin
brehn • veen

aquavit, grain or potato based spirit

bröd
br_urd_

bread

brödsmulor
brurd • smeu • lohr

bread crumbs

bröst
brurst

breast

buljong
buhl • _yong_

broth

bulle
buh • ler

bun

burköl
buhrk • url

canned beer

bål
boal

punch

böckling
burk • lihng

smoked herring

böna
bur • na

bean [pulses]

bönskott
burn • skoht

bean sprout

champinjon
sham • pihn • _yoan_

mushroom

chilipeppar
shee • lih • peh • par

chili pepper

chips
shihps

potato chips
[crisps]

choklad
shoa • klahd

chocolate

citron
see • troan

lemon

citronjuice
see • troan • yoas

lemon juice

cognac
kohn • yak

brandy

cola
koa • la

cola

dadel
dahd • ehl

date

dagens meny
dah • gehns meh • neu

menu of the day

dagens rätt
dah • gehns rairtt

speciality of the
day

dessertvin
deh • sair • veen

dessert wine

dillsås
dihl • soas

dill sauce

dragon
dra • goan

tarragon

dryck med alkohol
drewk meed al • ko • hoal

alcoholic drink

efterrätt
ehf • tehr • rairt

dessert

en halv flaska
ehn halv fla • ska

half bottle

enbär
een • bair

juniper berry

endiv
an • deev

endive

entrecote
an • treh • koa

sirloin steak

falukorv
fah • leu • kohrv

lightly spiced
sausage

fasan
fa • sahn

pheasant

fatöl
faht • url

draft [draught] beer

fikon
fee • kohn

fig

filé
fih • leh

filet mignon

filmjölk
feel • mjurlk

thick yogurt

fisk
fihsk

fish

fisk och skaldjur
fihsk • ohk • skahl • yeur

fish and seafood

fisksoppa
fihsk • sop • a

fish soup

fläsk
flehsk

pork

fläskben
flehsk • been

ham bone

fläskfilé
flehsk • fih • leh

fillet of pork

fläskkarré
flehsk • ka • reh

pork loin

fläskkorv
flehsk • kohrv

spicy, boiled pork
sausage

fläsklägg
flehsk • lehg

knuckle of pork

fläskpannkaka
flehsk • pan • kah • ka
thick pancake filled with bacon

forell
foa • _rehl_
trout

franskbröd
fransk • br**urd**
French bread

friterad camembert med hjortronsylt
free • _tee_ • rad cam • ehm • _behrt_ meed _yoh_ • tron • sewlt
deep-fried Camembert with cloudberry jam

frukost
fruh • _kohst_
breakfast

frukostflingor
fruhkost • flihng • ohr
(cold) cereal

frukt
fruhkt
fruit

fruktjuice
fruhkt • **yoa**s
fruit juice

fruktsallad
fruhkt • sal • ad
fruit salad

fullkornsmjöl
fuhl • kohrns • my**url**
whole wheat flour

fylld (med)
fewld (meed)
stuffed (with)

fylld oliv
fewld o • _leev_
stuffed olive

fylligt
few • liht
full-bodied (wine)

fågel
foa • gehl
poultry

får
foar
mutton

fårost
foar • oast
ewe's milk cheese

fänkål
fehn • koal
fennel

färsk (frukt)
fehrsk (fruhkt)
fresh (fruit)

färsk fikon
fairsk <u>fee</u> • kohn
fresh fig

färska räkor
<u>fairs</u> • ka <u>rair</u> • kohr
unshelled shrimp [prawns]

färskpotatis
<u>fairsk</u> • poa • <u>tah</u> • tihs
new potato

förlorat ägg
furr • <u>loa</u> • rat ehg
poached egg

förrätt
<u>furr</u> • rairt
appetizer [starter]

garnering
gar • <u>nee</u> • rihng
garnish

gelé
sheh • <u>leh</u>
jelly

get
yeet
kid (goat)

getost
<u>yeet</u> • oast
goat cheese

gin
jihn
gin

glass
glas
ice cream

glutenfritt
<u>glue</u> • tehn • friht
gluten free

glögg
gl<u>urg</u>
mulled wine with port and spices, served hot

grapefrukt
<u>grahp</u> • fruhkt
grapefruit

gratinerad
gra • tih • <u>nee</u> • rad
au gratin

gratäng
gra • <u>tehng</u>
casserole

gravlax
grafv • lax
marinated salmon

grevé
greh • veh
semi-hard cheese

grillad kyckling
grihl • ahd chewk • lihng
grilled chicken

grillspett
grihl • speht
skewer

gryta
grew • ta
pot roast, stew or casserole

grädde
greh • der
cream

gräddfil
grehd • feel
sour cream

gräslök
grairs • lurk
chive

grön böna
grur • na bur • na
green bean

grön paprika
grurn pah • pree • ka
green pepper

grön vindruva
grurn veen • dreu • va
green grape

grönsak
grurn • sahk
vegetable

grönsakssoppa
grurn • sahks • sohp • a
vegetable soup

grönsallad
grurn • sal • ad
green salad

gröt
grurt
(hot) cereal

gurka
geur • ka
cucumber

gås
goas
goose

gädda _yeh • da_	sea perch
hallon _hal • ohn_	raspberry
halstrad fisk _hal • strahd fihsk_	grilled fish
halstrad forell med färskpotatis _hal • strad foa • rehl med_ _fairsk • poa • tah • this_	grilled trout with new potatoes
hamburgare _ham • beur • ya • rer_	hamburger
hare _hah • rer_	rabbit
haricots verts _ar • ee • koh • vair_	string beans
hasselbackspotatis _ha • sehl • baks • poa • tah • tihs_	oven-baked potato, coated in bread crumbs
hasselnöt _ha • sehl • nurt_	hazelnut
havre _hafv • rer_	oats
havregryn _hafv • reh • greun_	oatmeal
havsabborre _hafs • a • boh • rer_	sea bass
hemlagad _hehm • lah • gad_	homemade
herrgårdsakvavit _hair • goards • a • kva • veet_	aquavit flavored with caraway seeds and whisky
herrgårdsost _hehr • goards • oast_	semi-hard cheese with a nutty flavor
hett _heht_	hot (temperature)

hjort	deer
yohrt	
hjortron	cloudberry
yoahr • tron	
hjortron sylt	cloudberry jam
yoar • trohn • sewlt	
honung	honey
hoa • neung	
hovmästarsås	dill sauce
hoav • mehs • tar • soas	
hummer	lobster
huhm • ehr	
husets specialitet	specialty of the house
heu • sehts speh • sih • al • ee • teet	
husets vin	house wine
heu • sehts veen	
huvudrätt	main course
heu • vuhd • rait	
hårdkokt ägg	hard-boiled egg
hoard • kohkt ehg	
hårt bröd	crispbread
hoart brurd	
hälleflundra	halibut
heh • leh • fleun • dra	
ingefära	ginger
ih • ng • eh • fai • ra	
inlagd i ättika (vinäger)	marinated in vinegar
ihn • lahgd ee eh • tih • ka	
inlagd sill	marinated (pickled) herring
ihn • lahgd sil	
is	ice
ees	
isterband	sausage of pork, barley and beef
ihs • tehr • band	

Janssons frestelse
yahn • sons _frehs_ • tehl • ser

casserole with potatoes and anchovies

jordgubbar med grädde
yoard • guhb • ar meed _greh_ • deh

strawberries and cream

jordgubbe
yoard • guh • ber

strawberry

jordnöt
yoard • nurt

peanut

juice
yoas

juice

julbord
yeul • board

buffet of hot and cold Swedish specialties served at Christmas time

kaffe
_ka_ • fer

coffee

kaka
kah • ka

cake

kalkon
kal • _koan_

turkey

kall soppa
kal _sohp_ • a

cold soup

kallskuret
kal • skeu • reht

cold cuts

kalops
ka • _lohps_

beef stew

kalvbräss
kalv • brehs

sweetbread

kalvkött
kalv • churt

veal

kalvsylta
kalv • sewl • ta

cold veal in jelly

kammussla
kam • muhs • la

scallop

kanderad frukt
kan • deeh • rahd fruhkt
candied fruit

kanel
ka • neel
cinnamon

kantarell
kan • ta • rehl
chanterelle
mushroom

kapris
ka • prees
caper

karaff
ka • raff
carafe

karameller
ka • ra • mehl • ehr
candy [sweets]

karré
ka • reh
tenderloin

katrinplommon
ka • treen • ploa • mohn
prune

kex
kehx
cookie [biscuit]

kikärta
cheek • air • ta
chickpea

kiwifrukt
kee • vee • fruhkt
kiwi

klimp
klihmp
dumpling

kokosnöt
koa • kos • nurt
coconut

kokt katrinplommon
koakt ka • treen • ploa • mohn
stewed prune

kokt potatis
koakt poa • tah • tihs
boiled potato

kokt skinka
koakt shihng • ka
boiled ham

kokt ägg
koakt ehg
boiled egg

kolja
kohl • ya

haddock

kolsyrad
koal • sew • rad

carbonated

kompott
kom • poht

stewed fruit

konserverad frukt
kon • ser • vee • rad fruhkt

canned fruit

korv
kohrv

sausage

kotlett
koht • lehtt

cutlet

krabba
kra • ba

crab

kronärtskocka
kroan • airts • koh • ka

artichoke

kroppkaka
kropp • kah • ka

potato dumpling,
filled with bacon
and onions

krusbär
kreus • bair

gooseberry

krydda
krew • da

spice

kryddad
krew • dad

spicy

kryddad pepparsås
krew • dahd peh • par • soas

hot pepper sauce

kryddost
krewd • oast

sharp, strong
cheese with
caraway seeds

kryddpeppar
krewd • peh • par

allspice

kryddstarkt
krewd • starkt

spicy

kräfta
krehf • ta

crayfish

kummel
keu • mel

hake

kummin
keu • meen

caraway

kvark
kvark

fresh curd cheese

kyckling
chewk • lihng

chicken

kycklingbröst
chewk • lihng • brurst

chicken breast

kycklinglever
chewk • lihng • lee • vehr

chicken liver

kycklingsoppa
chewk • lihng • sohp • a

chicken soup

kyld dryck
chewl drewk

cold drink

kylt
chewlt

chilled (wine, etc.)

kål
koal

cabbage

kåldolmar
koal • dohl • mar

cabbage leaves
stuffed with
chopped [minced]
meat and rice

kålrot
koal • roht

turnip

källkrasse
chehl • kra • se

watercress

körsbär
churs • bair

cherry

körvel
chur • vehl

chervil

kött
churt   meat

kött och grönsakssoppa   meat and
churt • oa • grurn • sahk • sohp • a   vegetable soup
                                soup

köttbulle   meatball
churt • buh • ler

köttfärs   chopped [minced]
churt • fairs   beef

köttsoppa   beef and vegetable
churt • sohp • a   soup with
                                dumplings

köttsås   meat sauce
churt • soas

lagerblad   bay leaf
lah • gehr • blahd

lageröl   lager
lah • ger • url

lamm   lamb
lamm

lammgryta   lamb stew
lamm • grew • ta

landgång   long open-faced
land • goang   sandwich

lax   salmon
lax

lever   liver
lee • vehr

leverpastej   liver pâté
lee • vehr pa • stay

lingon   lingonberry
lihng • ohn

lingonsylt   lingonberry jam
lihng • ohn • sewlt

lins
lihns
lentil

likör
lih • kurr
liqueur

lägg
lehg
shank (top of leg)

läsk
lehsk
soft drink

lättöl
leht • ur
light beer

löjrom
lury • rohm
bleak roe with chopped, raw onions and sour cream; served on toast

lök
lurk
onion

löksoppa
lurk • sohp • a
onion soup

lövbiff
lurv • bihf
fried, thinly sliced beef, with onions

majonnäs
may • oha • nairs
mayonnaise

majs
mays
sweet corn

makrill
mahk • rihl
mackerel

mandarin
man • da • reen
tangerine/ mandarin orange

mandel
man • dehl
almond

mandeltårta
man • dehl • toar • ta
almond tart

marmelad
mahr • meh • lahd
marmalade

marsipan
mahr • sih • pahn

marzipan

marulk
mahr • eulk

monkfish

maräng
mah • rehng

meringue

marängsviss
mah • rehng • svihs

meringue served
with cream and
chocolate sauce

matjesill
ma • shcheh • sihl

marinated herring

med citron
meed see • troan

with lemon

med florsocker
meed floar • soh • ker

with icing

med grädde
meed greh • der

with cream

med is
meed ees

with ice

med kolsyra
meed koal • sew • ra

carbonated (drink)

med mjölk
meed myurlk

with milk

med socker
meed soh • kehr

with sugar

med tonic
meed toh • nihk

with tonic water

med vatten
meed va • tehrn

with water

med vitlök
meed veet • lurk

with garlic

medaljong
meh • dal • yong

small fillet of cut
meat

medium
meh • dee • yuhm

medium

mellanmål
meh • lan • moal

snack

(vatten)melon
(va • tehrn)meh • loan

(water)melon

meny
meh • neu

menu

mesost
mees • oast

soft, sweet whey
cheese

middag
mih • dahg

dinner

milkshake
milk • shake

milk shake

mineralvatten
mih • neh • rahl • va • tehrn

mineral water

mjuk pepparkaka
myeuk peh • par • kah • ka

soft ginger cake

mjukost
myeuk • oast

soft cheese

mjöl
myurl

flour

mjölk
myurlk

milk

mogen
moa • gehn

ripe

morot
moa • roht

carrot

mousserande
moa • see • ran • der

sparkling (wine)

muffin
muh • fihn

muffin

mullbär
muhl • bair

mulberry

multe
muhl • ter

mullet

munk
muhnk
donut

muskot
muhs • koht
nutmeg

müsli
mews • lee
granola [muesli]

mussla
muhs • la
mussel

mustigt
muhs • tihkt
full-bodied (wine)

mycket kryddad
mew • keht krew • dad
highly seasoned

mycket torrt
mew • keht tohrt
very dry (wine, etc.)

mynta
mewn • ta
mint (herb)

mäktig
mehk • tihg
rich (sauce)

mördegstårta
muhr • deegs • toar • ta
tart (sweet or savory)

mört
murtt
roach (type of fish)

nejlika
nay • lih • ka
clove

nektarin
nehk • ta • reen
nectarine

njure
nyeu • rer
kidney

nudel
neu • dehl
noodle

nyponsoppa
new • pohn • sohp • a
rose-hip soup

nötkött
nurt • churt
red meat

odlade champinjon — cultivated mushroom
oad • lah • der sham • peen • _yoa_n

ojäst bröd — unleavened bread
oa • _yair_st br_urd_

oliv — olive
o • _leev_

olja och vinäger — oil and vinegar
oal • ya ohk vee • _nai_ • gehr

omelett — omelet
om • eh • _leht_

ost — cheese
oast

ostbricka — cheese plate
oast • brih • ka

ostkaka — curd cake served with jam
oast • kah • ka

ostkex — cheese cracker
oast • kehx

ostron — oyster
_oa_ • strohn

oxkött — ox
oax • churt

oxrullad — braised roll of beef
oax • reu • _lahd_

oxsvans — oxtail
oax • svans

oxsvanssoppa — oxtail soup
oax • svans • _sohp_ • a

paj — pie
pay

palsternacka — parsnip
pal • stehr • na • ka

pannbiff — beef patty
pan • bihf

pannkaka
pan • kah • ka

pancake

paprika
pah • prih • ka

pepper (fresh)

pasta
pas • ta

pasta

pastarätt
pas • ta • rairt

pasta dish

pastej
pa • stay

pâté

peppar
peh • par

pepper (condiment)

pepparkaka
peh • par • kah • ka

ginger cookie

pepparrotssås
peh • pa • roat • soas

horseradish sauce

persika
pair • shih • ka

peach

persilja
pair • shihl • ya

parsley

piggvar
pihg • vahr

turbot

pitabröd
pee • ta • brurd

pita bread

plommon
ploa • mohn

plum

plättar
pleh • tar

small pancakes
served with jam
and whipped cream

pomegranat äpple
pom • eh • gra • naht • ehp • leh

pomegranate

pommes frites
pohm • friht

French fries

portion
pohrt • shoan

portion

portvin
pohrt • veen
port

potatis
poa • _tah_ • tihs
potato

potatismos
poa • _tah_ • tihs • moas
mashed potatoes

potatissoppa
poa • _tah_ • tihs • _sohp_ • a
potato soup

prinsesstårta
prihn • _sehs_ • _toar_ • ta
sponge cake with (vanilla) custard, whipped cream and jam, covered in light green marzipan

prinskorv
prihns • kohrv
small pork sausage

prästost
prehst • oast
hard cheese with a strong, rich flavor

pumpa
puhm • pa
pumpkin

punsch
peunsh
sweet liqueur

purjolök
peur • yoh • lurk
leek

pytt i panna
pewt • ee • pa • na
chunks of fried meat, onion and potatoes

på beställning
poa beh • _stehl_ • nihng
made on request

pärlande
pair • lan • der
sparkling

pärlhöns
pairl • hurns
guinea fowl

päron
pai • rohn
pear

rabarber	rhubarb
rah • bar • behr	
ragu	beef stew
ra • gue	
rapphöna	partridge
rap • hurna	
ren	reindeer
reen	
renat	flavorless, clear
ree • nat	spirit (aquavit)
renstek	roast reindeer
reen • steek	
revbensspjäll	spare ribs
reev • beens • spehl	
riktigt blodig	very rare
rihk • tihgt bloa • dihg	
rimmad lax	lightly salted
rih • mad lax	salmon
ris	rice
rees	
rocka	ray (type of fish)
roh • ka	
rom	rum
rohm	
rosé	blush (wine)
roh • seh	
rosmarin	rosemary
roas • ma • reen	
rostat bröd	toast
rohs • tat brurd	
rostbiff	roast beef
rohst • bihf	
rova	turnip
roa • va	

rumpstek
ruhmp • steek

rump steak

russin
ruh • sihn

raisin

rå
roa

raw

rådjur
roa • yeur

venison

rådjursstek
roa • yeur • steek

roast of venison

rågbröd
roag • brurd

rye bread

rädisa
raid • dih • sa

radish

räkor
rair • kohr

shrimp [prawns]

rätt
reht

dish

röd paprika
rurd _pah_ • pree • ka

sweet red pepper

röd vinbär
rurd _veen_ • bair

red currant

rödbeta
rurd • bee • ta

beet

röding
rur • dihng

char

rödkål
rurd • koal

red cabbage

rödspätta
rurd • speh • ta

plaice

rökt fisk
rurkt fisk

smoked fish

rökt lax
rurkt lax

smoked salmon

rökt renstek
rurkt reen • steek
smoked reindeer

rökt skinka
rurkt shihng • ka
smoked ham

rökt ål
rurkt oal
smoked eel

rörd soppa
rurrd sohp • a
cream soup

rött
rurt
red (wine)

sadel
sah • dehl
saddle (cut of meat)

saffransbullar
sa • frans • buh • lar
Christmas saffron buns

saft
saft
squash (fruit cordial)

salamikorv
sa • lah • mee • kohrv
salami

sallad
sal • ad
salad

salladshuvud
sal • ads • heu • vuhd
head of lettuce

salt
salt
salt

saltade jordnötter
sal • ta • der yoard • nur • ter
salted peanuts

saltgurka
salt • geur • ka
salted, pickled gherkin

salvia
sal • vee • a
sage

sardin
sar • deen
sardine

schalottenlök
sha • loh • tehn • lurk
shallot

schnitzel
shniht • sehl

escallope

selleri
seh • leh • ree

celery

senap
see • nap

mustard

sherry
sheh • ree

sherry

sill
sihl

herring

sillbricka
sihl • brih • ka

variety of
marinated herring

sillsallad
sihl • sal • ad

beet and herring
salad

sirap
seh • rap

syrup

sjömansbiff
shur • mans • bihf

casserole of fried
beef, onions and
potatoes, braised
in beer

sjötunga
sjur • teung • a

sole

skaldjur
skahl • yeur

shellfish

skaldjurssallad
skahl • yeurs • sal • ad

shellfish salad

skarpsill
skarp • sihl

herring

skinka
skihng • ka

ham

skogssvamp
skoags • svamp

field mushroom

sky
shewy

gravy

skåne
skoa • ner

type of aquavit
flavored with
aniseed and
caraway

smultron
smeul • trohn

wild strawberry

småbröd
smoa • brurd

roll

småkaka
smoa • kah • ka

cookie [biscuit]

smårätt
smoa • rairt

snack

småsill
smoa • sihl

herring

smör
smur

butter

smördeg
smur • deeg

pastry

smörgås
smur • goas

Swedish open-
faced sandwich

snigel
sneeg • ehl

snail

socker
soh • kehr

sugar

sockerdricka
soh • kehr • drih • ka

lemonade

sockerkaka
soh • kehr • kah • ka

sponge cake

sockerärta
soh • kehr • air • ta

sugar snap pea
[mangetout]

sodavatten
soa • da • va • tehrn

soda water

soppa
sohp • a

soup

S.O.S. (smör, ost och sill)
ehs oa ehs (smur oast ohk sihl)

small plate of marinated herring, read, butter and cheese

sparris
spar • ihs

asparagus

sparrissoppa
spa • rihs • sohp • a

asparagus soup

specialitet för landsdelen
speh • sih • ahl • ih • teet furr lands • deel • ehn

local specialty

spenat
speh • naht

spinach

spenatsoppa
speh • naht • sohp • a

spinach soup

sprit
spreet

spirits

spädgris
spaird • grees

unweaned piglet

squash
skoawsh

squash (vegetable)

stark
stark

strong (flavor)

starkt kryddad
starkt krew • dad

hot (spicy)

stek
steek

roast

stekt fisk
steekt fisk

fried fish

stekt kyckling
steekt chewk • lihng

fried chicken (not breaded)

stekt potatis
steekt poa • tah • tihs

sautéed potato

stekt ägg
steekt ehg

fried egg

strömming
strurm • ihng

sprats (small Baltic herring)

strömmingsflundra
strurm • ihngs • fleun • dra

Baltic herring, filleted and sandwiched in pairs, fried, with dill and butter filling

stuvad abborre
st**eu** • vad **a** • bohr • er

perch poached with onion, parsley and lemon

sufflé
suh • fleh

soufflé

sultana
suhl • tahn • a

sultana raisin

sur
seur

sour

svamp
svamp

mushroom

svart vinbär
svart veen • bair

black currant

svecia
sveh • see • a

semi-hard cheese

svensk punsch
sven • sk peunsh

Swedish punch (sweet liqueur)

sylt
sewlt

jam

sås
_s**oa**s_

sauce

sötningsmedel
surt • nihngs • mee • dehl

artificial sweetener

sötpotatis
surt • poa • tah • tihs

sweet potato

sötsur sås
surt • seur s**oa**s

sweet-and-sour sauce

sött
suht
sweet

T-benstek
tee • been • steek
T-bone steak

thé
tee
tea

timjan
tihm • yan
thyme

toast skagen
toast skah • gehn
toast with chopped
shrimp in
mayonnaise,
topped with bleak
roe

tomat
toa • maht
tomato

tomater och lök
toa • mah • ter ohk lurk
tomato and onion
salad

tomatjuice
toa • maht • yoas
tomato juice

tomatsoppa
toa • maht • soh • pa
tomato soup

tomatsås
toa • maht • soas
tomato sauce

tonfisk
toan • fihsk
tuna

tonic
toh • nihk
tonic water

torkade dadel
tohr • ka • der dah • dehl
dried date

torkade fikon
tohr • ka • der fee • kohn
dried fig

torrt
tohrt
dry

torsk
torshk
cod

tunga
tuhng • a
tongue (cow)

tunn sås
tuhnn soas
light (sauce)

tunnbröd
tuhnn • brurd
Swedish flat bread, can be soft or crispy

tårta
toarta
sponge-based fruit or cream cake

ugnsbakad fisk
eungns • bah • kad fihsk
oven-baked fish

ugnsstekt kyckling
eungn • steekt chewk • lihng
roast chicken

ugnsstekt potatis
eungn • steekt poa • tah • tihs
roast potato

utan koffein
eu • tan ko • feen
decaffeinated

vaktel
vak • tehl
quail

valfria tillbehör
vahl • free • a tihl • beh • hurr
choice of side dishes

valnöt
vahl • nurt
walnut

vanilj
va • nihly
vanilla

vaniljsås
va • nihly • soas
vanilla sauce, often like custard

varmchoklad
varm shoa • klahd
hot chocolate

varmkorv
varm kohrv
hot dog

varmrätt
varm • rairt
warm meal, usually main course

varmt
varmt
hot

vatten
va • tehrn
water

vattenkrasse
va • tehrn • kra • ser
watercress

vaxböna
vax • bur • na
butter bean

vegetarisk meny
vehg • eh • tah • risk meh • neu
vegetarian menu

vermouth
vehr • meutt
vermouth

vetemjöl
vee • teh • mjurl
wheat flour (regular)

whisky
vihs • kee
whisky

wienerbröd
vee • nehr • brurd
Danish pastry

wienerschnitzel
vee • nehr • shniht • sehl
breaded veal cutlet

vild champinjon
vihl • da sham • pihn • yoan
wild mushroom

vildand
vihld • and
wild duck

vilt
vihlt
game

viltpastej
vihlt • pa • stay
game pâté

vin
veen
wine

vinaigrettesås
vih • neh • greht • soas
vinaigrette [French dressing]

vinbär
veen • bair
currant

vindruva
veen • dreu • va
grape

vinlista _veen_ • lihs • ta	wine list
vispgrädde _visp_ • greh • der	whipped cream
vit sås veet soas	white sauce
vitkål _veet_ • koal	white cabbage
vitkålssallad _veet_ • koal • sal • ad	coleslaw
vitling _veet_ • lihng	whiting
vitlök _veet_ • lurk	garlic
vitlöksmajonnäs _veet_ • lurks • may • oa • _nairs_	garlic mayonnaise
vitlökssås _veet_ • lurk • soas	garlic sauce
vinbär _veen_ • bair	currant
vindruva _veen_ • dreu • va	grape
vinlista _veen_ • lihs • ta	wine list
vispgrädde _visp_ • greh • der	whipped cream
vitt viht	white (wine)
vitt bröd viht brurd	white bread
vodka _vod_ • ka	vodka
vol au vent vohl • oa • _vahnt_	vol-au-vent (pastry filled with meat or fish)

våffla (med sylt och grädde)
vohf • la meed sewlt ohk greh • der
waffle (with jam and whipped cream)

vårlök
voar lurk
shallot [spring onion]

västerbotten
vehs • tehr • boh • tehn
strong, tangy, hard cheese

västkustsallad
vehst • kuhst • sal • ad
west coast salad, with shrimp [prawns] and mussels

yoghurt
yoa • geurt
yogurt

zucchini
seu • kee • nee
zucchini [courgette]

ål
oal
eel

ångkokt fisk
oang • koakt fisk
steamed fish

ädelost
air • dehl • oast
blue cheese

ägg
ehg
egg

äggplanta
ehg • plan • ta
eggplant [aubergine]

äggula
ehg • geu • la
egg yolk

äggröra
ehg • rur • ra
scrambled egg

äggvita
ehg • vee • ta
egg white

älg
ehly
moose

älgfilé
ehly • fih • leh
fillet of moose

älgstek _ehly_ • steek	moose roast
älgstek med svampsås _ehly_ • steek meed _svamp_ • s**oa**s	roast moose with mushroom sauce
äppelkaka _eh_ • pehl • _kah_ • ka	apple cake
äppelpaj _ehp_ • ehl • _pay_	apple tart
äppelring _ehp_ • ehl • _rihng_	apple fritter
äpple _ehp_ • leh	apple
ärta _air_ • ta	pea
ärtsoppa _airt_ • sohp • a	green or yellow pea soup
ättiksgurka _eh_ • tihks • geur • ka	sweet, pickled gherkins
öl ur**l**	beer
öl på flaska ur**l** poa _fla_ • ska	bottled beer

GOING OUT

GOING OUT

NEED TO KNOW

Do you have a program of events?	**Har ni ett evenemangsprogram?** *hahr nee eht eh • vehn • eh • <u>mangs</u> • proa • gram*
What's playing at the movies [cinema] tonight?	**Vad visas på bio ikväll?** *vahd <u>vee</u> • sas poa <u>bee</u> • oa ee • <u>kvehl</u>*
Where's...?	**Var ligger...?** *vahr <u>lih</u> • gehr...*
the downtown area	**centrum** *<u>sehn</u> • truhm*
the bar	**baren** *<u>bah</u> • rehn*
the dance club	**diskoteket** *dis • koh • <u>tee</u> • keht*

ENTERTAINMENT

Can you recommend...?	**Kan du rekommendera...?** *kan deu reh • koh • mehn • <u>dee</u> • ra...*
a concert	**en konsert** *ehn kohn • <u>sair</u>*
a movie	**en film** *ehn film*
an opera	**en opera** *ehn <u>oa</u> • peh • ra*
a play	**en teaterpjäs** *ehn tee • <u>ah</u> • tehr • pjais*

When does it start/ end?	**När börjar/slutar den?**
	nair bur • yar/sleu • tar dehn
What's the dress code?	**Vilken klädsel gäller?**
	vihl • kehn klaid • sehl gehl • lehr
I like…	**Jag tycker om…**
	yahg tew • kehr ohm…
classical music	**klassisk musik**
	klas • isk meu • seek
folk music	**folkmusik**
	folk • meu • seek
jazz	**jazz**
	yas
pop music	**popmusik**
	pop • meu • seek
rap	**rap**
	rap

For Tickets, see page 45.

YOU MAY HEAR…

Stäng av mobiltelefonen, tack.
stehng afv
mo • beel • teh • leh • foa • nen tak

Turn off your
cell [mobile]
phones, please.

NIGHTLIFE

What's there to do at night?	**Vad kan man göra på kvällarna?** *vahd kan man yur•ra poa kvehl•ar•na*
Can you recommend...?	**Kan du rekommendera...?** *kan deu reh•koh•mehn•dee•ra...*
a bar	**en bar** *ehn bahr*
a casino	**ett kasino** *eht ka•see•noh*
a dance club	**ett diskotek** *eht dis•koh•tehk*
a gay club	**en gayklubb** *ehn gay•kluhb*
a jazz club	**en jazzklubb** *ehn yas•kluhb*
a club with local music	**en klubb med lokal musik** *ehn kluhb meed lo•kahl meu•seek*
a nightclub	**en nattklubb** *ehn nat•kluhb*
Is there live music?	**Spelar man livemusik där?** *spee•lar man live•meu•seek dair*
How do I get there?	**Hur kan jag komma dit?** *heur kan yahg koh•ma deet*
Is there a cover charge?	**Är det kuvertavgift?** *air de keu•vair•afv•yihft*
Let's go dancing.	**Vi går ut och dansar.** *vee goar eut ohk dan•sar*
Is this area safe at night?	**Är detta område säkert på natten?** *ehr deh•ta ohm•roh•deh seh•kehrt poh na•tehn*

Sweden has produced several world famous pop and rock bands, and music is an important part of contemporary culture and entertainment. The government generously supports independent musicians, as well as smaller music groups, orchestras and symphonies. In larger cities and towns you'll easily find concerts and performances to attend, and information should be listed at the tourist office or its webpage regarding upcoming concerts and events. If you are traveling in Sweden during the summer, attending a music festival is an unforgettable experience. **The Peace & Love Festival** in Borlänge, just two hours from Stockholm, is popular among the younger crowd. Stockholm is home to **Ung08**, which is Europe's largest youth festival, geared toward 13-19 year olds. **The Hultsfred Festival**, in southern Sweden, is the oldest and largest festival. There are also a host of other music festivals covering everything from folk music, to pop and jazz.

ROMANCE

NEED TO KNOW

Would you like to go out for a drink/dinner?	**Har du lust att ta en drink/gå ut och äta?**
	hahr deu luhst at tah ehn drihnk/goa eut ohk air • ta
What are your plans for tonight/tomorrow?	**Vad har du för planer för ikväll/imorgon?**
	vahd hahr deu furr plah • nehr furr ee • kvehl/ee • mo • ron
Can I have your number?	**Kan jag få ditt telefonnummer?**
	kan yahg foa diht teh • leh • foan • nuhm • ehr
May I join you?	**Får jag göra dig sällskap?**
	foar yahg yurra dihg sehl • skahp
Can I buy you a drink?	**Får jag bjuda på en drink?**
	foar yahg byeu • da poa ehn drihnk
I like you.	**Jag gillar dig.**
	yahg yihl • ar day
I love you.	**Jag älskar dig.**
	yahg ehl • skar day

THE DATING GAME

Would you like to…?	**Har du lust att…?**
	hahr deu luhst at…
go out for coffee	**gå ut och ta en kopp kaffe**
	goa eut ohk tah ehn kohp ka • fer

go for a drink	**ta en drink**
	tah ehn drihnk
go out for a meal	**gå ut och äta**
	goa eut ohk <u>air</u> • ta
What are your plans for...?	**Vad har du för planer för...?**
	vahd hahr deu furr <u>plah</u> • nehr furr...
today	**idag**
	ee • dahg
tonight	**ikväll**
	ee • <u>kvehl</u>
tomorrow	**imorgon**
	ee • <u>mo</u> • ron
this weekend	**den här helgen**
	dehn hair <u>hehl</u> • yehn
Where would you like to go?	**Vart vill du gå?**
	vart vihl deu goa
I'd like to go to...	**Jag skulle vilja gå till.**
	yahg <u>skuh</u> • ler vihl • ya goa tihl...
Do you like...?	**Tycker du om...?**
	<u>tew</u> • kehr deu ohm...
Can I have your number/e-mail?	**Kan jag få ditt nummer/din e-post?**
	kan yahg foa diht <u>nuhm</u> • ehr/dihn ee • <u>pohst</u>
Are you on Facebook/ Twitter?	**Finns du på Facebook/Twitter?**
	fihns deu poa Facebook/Twitter
Can I join you?	**Får jag följa med?**
	foar yahg <u>furl</u> • ya meed
You're very attractive.	**Du är väldigt snygg.**
	deu air vehl • dihkt snewgg
You look great!	**Vad du ser vacker ut!**
	vahd deu seer <u>va</u> • kehr eut
Shall we go somewhere quieter?	**Ska vi gå till ett lugnare ställe?**
	skah vee goa tihl eht <u>luhng</u> • na • rer <u>stehl</u> • ler

For Communications, see page 84.

ACCEPTING & REJECTING

Thank you. I'd love to.	**Tack, det vill jag gärna.** *tak dee vihl yahg yair • na*
Where should we meet?	**Var ska vi träffas?** *vahr skah vee treh • fas*
I'll meet you at the bar/your hotel.	**Vi träffas i baren/på ditt hotell.** *vee treh • fas ee bahr • en/poa diht hoh • tehl*
I'll come by at…	**Jag kommer…** *yahg koh • mehr…*
What's your address?	**Vilken address har du?** *Vihl • kehn ahd • rehs hahr deu*
Thank you, but I'm busy.	**Tack, men jag är upptagen.** *tak men yahg air uhp • tah • gehn*
I'm not interested.	**Jag är inte intresserad.** *yahg air in • ter in • treh • see • rad*
Leave me alone, please!	**Kan du lämna mig ifred, tack!** *kan deu lehm • na may ee • freed tak*
Stop bothering me!	**Sluta störa mig!** *sluh • ta stur • ra may*

GETTING INTIMATE

Can I hug/kiss you?	**Får jag krama/kysa dig?**
	foar yahg <u>krah</u> • ma/<u>chews</u> • a day
Yes.	**Ja.**
	yah
No.	**Nej.**
	nay
Stop!	**Stopp!**
	stop

SEXUAL PREFERENCES

Are you gay?	**Är du gay?**
	air deu gay
I'm…	**Jag är…**
	yahg air…
heterosexual	**heterosexuell**
	<u>heh</u> • tehr • ro • sehk • shew • <u>ehl</u>
homosexual	**homosexuell**
	<u>hoh</u> • moa • sehk • shew • <u>ehl</u>
bisexual	**bisexuell**
	<u>bee</u> • sehk • shew • <u>ehl</u>
Do you like men/ women?	**Gillar du män/kvinnor?**
	yih • lahr deu mehn/kvih • nohr

For Grammar, see page 14.

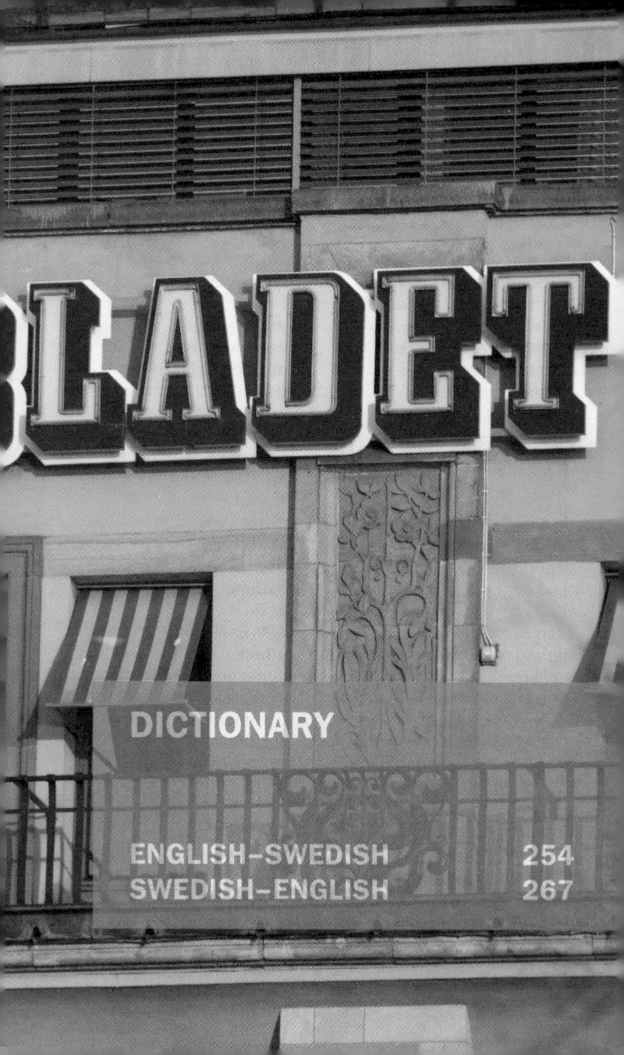

DICTIONARY

ENGLISH–SWEDISH

A

about (approximately) omkring
accept v acceptera
accident olycka
accommodation logi
acetaminophen paracetamol
across över
acupuncture akupunktur
adapter adapter
address n adress
adopt v adoptera
after efter
age ålder
air conditioning luftkonditionering
air mail flygpost
airline flygbolag
airport flygplats
aisle seat plats i mittgången
all alla
allergic allergisk
allergic reaction allergisk reaktion
allergy allergi
allow v tillåta
alter v ändra på
alternate route annan väg
aluminum foil aluminiumfolie
a.m. fm
ambulance ambulans
amount summa
amusement park nöjesfält
and och

anemic anemisk
animal djur
another annan
antiques store antikaffär
antiseptic cream antiseptisk salva
anyone någon
anything något
apartment lägenhet
apologize v be om ursäkt
appliance apparat
approve v godkänna
area code riktnummer
aromatherapy aroma-terapi
arrival ankomst
arrive v anlända
ask v fråga
aspirin huvudvärkstablett
asthma astma
at vid
ATM Bankomat
attack n anfall
audio guide audioguide
authentic äkta
automatic automatisk
available ledig
away iväg

B

baby baby
baby bottle nappflaska
baby formula välling
baby wipes våtservetter för barn

---

adj adjective	BE British English	v verb
adv adverb	n noun	

babysitter barnvakt
backpack ryggsäck
bad dålig
bag (shopping) påse
baggage cart bagagekärra
baggage claim bagageutlämning
bakery bageri
band (music group) band
bandage (gauze) gasbinda
bank bank
bank charge bankavgift
banknote sedel
bar bar
barber herrfrisör
bath bad
bathroom badrum; **(toilet)** toalett
battery batteri
battlefield slagfält
be v vara
beach strand
beautiful vacker
become v bli
bed n säng
before före
begin v börja
behind bakom
belt skärp
between mellan
big stor
bicycle cykel
bicycle lock cykelås
bikini bikini
bill n **(restaurant bill)** nota;
   (hotel, invoice) räkning
birthday födelsedag
bite n bett; v **(bite)** bita; v **(chew)**
   tugga
black svart
blanket n täcke
bleed v blöda
blood blod
blood pressure blodtryck

blouse blus
board v **(flight)** borda
boarding house pensionat
boarding pass (airport)
   boardingkort
boat båt
boat tour båttur
book bok
bookstore bokhandel
boots stövlar
boring trist
botanical garden botanisk
   trädgård
bottle flaska
bottle opener flasköppnare
bowl djup tallrik
boy pojke
boyfriend pojkvän
bra behå
bracelet armband
break v gå sönder
breakdown v **(car)** gå sönder
breastfeed v amma
breathe andas
bridge bro
bring ta med
broken (broken) sönder;
   (damaged) trasig
brooch brosch
broom sopborste
brown brun
burn v brinna
bus buss
bus route busslinje
bus station bussterminal
bus stop busshållplats
business center businesscenter
business hours öppettider
business trip affärsresa
busy upptagen
but men
buy v köpa

C

cabin stuga
cafe kafé
calender kalender
call v (phone) ringa
calm lugn
camera kamera
camping bed tältsäng
can n burk; v (be able to) kan
can opener konservöppnare
cancel v avbeställa
car bil
car deck (ferry) bildäck
car ferry bilfärja
car park [BE] parkeringsplats
car rental biluthyrning
car seat bilbarnstol
carafe karaff
card n kort
carry on n (luggage) handbagage
cash kontant
cashier (male) kassör; (female)
   kassörska
casino kasino
castle slott
cathedral katedral
cave grotta
cell phone mobiltelefon
ceramics keramik
certificate of authenticity
   äkthetsbevis
chair lift stollift
change n (money) växel; v
   (transportation; a baby) byta; v
   (reservation) ändra;
cheap billig
check in v checka in
check in desk (airport)
   incheckning
check out v checka ut
checking account checkkonto

chemical toilet kemisk toalett
chemist [BE] apotek
chest bröstet
child barn
child's cot [BE] barnsäng
children's menu barnmeny
church kyrka
cigar cigarr
cinema [BE] bio
city (city) stad; (downtown)
   centrum
city map stadskarta
classical music klassiskmusik
clean n ren
cleaning supplies städutrustning
clear v (computer) rensa
cliff klippa
cling film [BE] plastfolie
clock klocka
close v stänga
closed stängt
clothing store klädaffär
coat rock
coffee shop konditori
coin mynt
cold (illness) förskylning;
   (temperature) kall
colleague kollega
color färg
comb kam
come v komma
company (business) firma;
   (companionship) sällskap
computer dator
concert konsert
conditioner hårbalsam
condom kondom
conference konferens
conference room konferensrum
confirm v (reservation) bekräfta
contact lens solution
   kontaktlinsvätska

contain *v* innehålla
contraceptive preventivmedel
convention hall kongresshall
cooking facilities kokmöjligheter
cool (temperature) sval
copy *n* kopia
copy machine kopieringsautomat
corkscrew korkskruv
correct rätt
cost *v* kosta
cotton bomull
cough *n* hosta; *v* hosta
country code landsnummer
cover charge kuvertavgift
credit card kreditkort
crib barnsäng
cross country skiing längdåkning
crystal (glass) kristallglas
cup kopp
culture kultur
currency valuta
currency exchange office
  växelkontor
customs tull
customs declaration form
  tulldeklaration
cute *adj* gullig
cycling cykelåkning

D

dala horse dalahäst
damage *v* (damage) skada; *n*
  (harm) skada
dance *v* dansa
dance club diskotek
day ticket dagsbiljett
day trip dagstur
deaf döv
debit card bankkort
declare *v* (customs) förtulla
deck chair solstol
deep djup

delay *n* försening
delete *v* (computer) radera
delicatessen delikatessaffär
denim denim
dentist tandläkare
denture tandprotes
deodorant deodorant
depart *v* (train) avgå
department store varuhus
departure (airport) avgång
departure gate avgångsgate
deposit handpenning
desire *adj* gärna; *n* lust
detour trafikomläggning
develop *v* (photos) framkalla
diabetic *n* diabetiker
dial *v* (number) slå
diamond diamant
diaper blöja
diarrhea diarré
diesel diesel
difficult svårt
digital digital
digital print digitalt kort
dirty smutsig
disabled rörelsehindrad
disabled accessible toilet [BE]
  handicappanpassad toalett
discount rabatt
discount card rabattkort
dish detergent diskmedel
dishwasher diskmaskin
display case vitrin
disposable camera
  engångskamera
disturb *v* störa
dive *v* dyka
divide *v* dela
diving equipment
  dykarutrustning
divorced skild
dizzy yr

do *v* (**do something**) göra; (**work with**) syssla med
do not disturb var god stör ej
doctor doktor
doll docka
dollar dollar
domestic (travel) inrikes
domestic flight inrikes flyg
domestic partner sambo
door dörr
dosage dosering
downtown centrum
dress klänning
dress code klädsel
drive *v* köra
driver's license körkort
drops (medication) droppar
dry cleaner kemtvätt
dubbed dubbad
duty free taxfri
duty free good taxfri vara

E

each varje
ear öra
earring örhänge
east öster
easy lätt
eat *v* äta
economy class turist klass
electrical outlet nätuttag
elevator hiss
e-mail e-post
e-mail address e-postadress
emergency nödsituation
emergency brake nödbroms
emergency exit nödutgång
English engelska
engrave *v* gravera
enter *n* (entrance) ingång; (computer) enter
entertainment underhållning

equipment utrustning
escalator rulltrappa
e-ticket e-biljett
European Union (EU) europeiska unionen
event händelse
examine *v* (medical) undersöka
excess baggage överviktsbagage
exchange rate växelkursen
excuse me (attention, pardon) ursäkta; (to get past) ursäkta mig
exit *n* (way out) utgång
expensive dyr
expert avancerad
express express
express mail expresspost
extension (phone) anknytning
eyeglasses glasögon

F

fabric tyg
family familj
fan (ventilation) fläkt
fantastic *adj* fantastisk
fare biljettpris
farm bondgård
fast fort
fax fax
fax machine fax machine
female kvinna
ferry färja
fever feber
field fält
fill *v* (prescription) göra i ordning
filling (dental) plomb
film [BE] film
fire exit brandutgång
first första
fishing fiske
fit *v* (clothing) passa
fitting room provrum

fix *v* laga
fixed price fast pris
flat [BE] lägenhet
flight flyg
flight number flygnummer
floor (level) våning
football [BE] fotboll
for (someone) för
foreign currency utländsk valuta
forest skog
forget *v* glömma
fork gaffel
form *n* blankett
fountain fontän
free (available) ledig
free of charge gratis
freezer frys
friend vän
from ifrån
frying pan stekpanna
fun rolig
function *v* (work) fungera
further (more) ytterligare

G

game spel
garbage sopor
garbage bag soppåse
gasoline bensin
gas station bensinstation
gate (boarding) gate
genuine äkta
get off (train) stiga av
gift shop presentaffär
gift present
girlfriend flickvän
give *v* ge
glass (drinking) glas
gold guld
golf golf
golf club golfklubba
golf course golfbana

good *adj* bra
goodbye hej då
greengrocer [BE] livsmedelsaffär
grocery store livsmedelsaffär
group grupp
guest gäst
guide (brochure) guide; (person) guide
guide dog ledarhund
gym gym

H

hair cut klippning
hair dryer hårtork
hair style frisyr
hairbrush hårborste
hairdresser damfrisör
hairspray hårspray
half halv
handbag [BE] handväska
handicapped rörelsehindrade
handicapped accessible toilet handicappanpassad toalett
handicraft hantverk
handmade handgjord
hat hatt
have *v* ha
health food store hälsokostaffär
hearing impaired hörselskadad
heat värme
helmet hjälm
help *n* hjälp; *v* hjälpa
here här
hi hej
highchair barnstol
highway motorväg
hike *v* vandra
hiking vandring
hill kulle
hire *v* [BE] rent
holiday [BE] (vacation) semester
holiday (celebration) helgdag

horseback riding ridsport
hospital sjukhus
hot varm
hotel hotell
hour timme
husband man

I

ibuprofen ibuprofen
ice hockey ishockey
identification (idenitification)
    legitimation; (ID card) ID-kort
ill [BE] sjuk
in i
included (in the price) inkluderad
indoor pool inomhusbassäng
information desk information
innocent oskyldig
insect insekt
insect bite insektbett
insect repellent mygg olja
inside inuti
instant messenger instant
    messenger
instructor instruktör
insurance försäkring
interesting intressant
international (travel) utrikes
international driver's license
    internationellt körkort
internet internet
internet cafe internetkafé
interpreter tolk
iron n (clothes) strykjärn; v
    (clothes) stryka
itemized bill specificerad räkning

J

jacket jacka
jeans jeans
jet ski jetski
jeweler juvelerare
jewelry smycken

job jobb

K

keep v behålla
key nyckel
key card nyckelkort
kiddie pool barnbassäng
kiss v kyssa
kitchen kök
knife kniv
krona (Swedish currency) krona

L

lace spets
lactose intolerant laktosinterant
ladies' restroom damtoilett
ladieswear damkläder
lake sjö
last sista
late sen
launderette [BE] snabbtvätt
laundromat snabbtvätt
laundry tvätt
laundry detergent tvättmedel
laundry facilities tvättmöjligheter
lawyer advokat
leather läder
leave v lämna
left (direction) vänster
lesson lektion
letter brev
library bibliotek
life boat livbåt
life jacket flytväst
lifeguard livräddare
lift (ski) lift
lift [BE] n (elevator) hiss
lift pass liftkort
light (lamp) lampa
light bulb glödlampa
lighter tändare
like v gilla

line (bus) linje
linen linne
live v bo
loafers loafers
lock v låsa
log on logga in
log out logga ut
long adj lång; adv länge
lose v (lost luggage) förlora; v
(drop, lose) tappa
lost n vilse
lost property office [BE]
hittegodsexpedition
lost and found
hittegodsexpedition
lottery lotto
love v älska
luggage locker förvaringsskåp

M

mail post
mailbox postlåda
manager chef
manicure manikyr
many många
map karta
market marknad
married gift
mass mässan
match (fire) tändsticka
meal måltid
mean v (signify) betyda
measuring spoon måttsked
medicine medicin
medium medium
meet v träffa
meeting sammanträde
memory card minneskort
men's restroom herrtoalett
menstrual cramps mensvärk
menstruation mens
menswear herrkläder

menu meny
message meddelande
microwave mikrovågsugn
minimum minimum
Miss fröken
mistake misstag
mobile phone [BE] mobiltelefon
moment ögonblick
mop n skurmop
moped moped
mosque moské
motel motell
motion sickness åksjuka
motorboat motorbåt
motorcycle motocykel
motorway [BE] motorväg
mountain berg
mouth mun
movie film
movies bio
Mr. herr
Mrs. fru
mugging överfall
multi-day card flerdagskort
museum museum
must måste

N

nail file nagelfil
nail salon nagelvårdssalong
name n namn
napkin servett
nappy [BE] blöja
nature reserve naturreservat
nearby nära
necklace halsband
need v behöva
new ny
newspaper tidning
newsstand tidningskiosk
next nästa
next to bredvid

nice *adj* snäll
no (not allowed) ej
nobody ingen
no smoking rökning förbjuden
north norr
not inte
not included (in the price) inte
  inkluderad
nothing inget
number nummer
nurse sjuksköterska

O

off av
old gammal
on (switch) på
one way (street) enkelriktad
one-way ticket enkel biljett
only bara
open *n* öppet; *v* öppna
opening hours [BE] öppettider
opera opera
opposite mitt emot
optician optiker
or eller
orchestra orkester
order *v* beställa
other andra
outdoor utomhus
outdoor pool utomhusbassäng
outside ute
overnight delivery (mail)
  expressutdelning
oxygen treatment
  syrebehandling

P

pacifier napp
package paket
paddling pool [BE] barnbassäng
pajamas pyjamas
panorama panorama

pants byxor
panty hose strumpbyxor
paper napkin papperservett
parcel [BE] paket
park *n* park; *v* parkera
parking parkering
parking lot parkeringsplats
passport pass
passport control passkontroll
password (computer) lösenord
pay phone telefonautomat
pay *v* betala
peak (mountain) top
pearl pärla
pedestrian crossing
  övergångsställe för fotgängare
pedestrian fotgängare
pedicure pedikyr
pen kulspetspenna
per per
per day per dag
per week per vecka
performance (music, theater)
  föreställning
person person
petite petit
petrol [BE] bensin
petrol station [BE] bensinstation
pewter tenn
pharmacy apotek
phone call samtal
phone card telefonkort
phone number telefonnummer
photo foto
pick up *v* (person/thing) hämta
picnic area picknickområde
piece bit
pill tablett
pillow kudde
PIN PIN kod
pink rosa
piste [BE] spår

place n ställe
plan n plan
plaster [BE] plåster
plastic wrap plastfolie
platform (train) plattform
platinum platina
plate tallrik
play n (theater) teaterpjäs;v spela
playground lekplats
playpen lekrum
pleasant trevlig
please (request) snälla;
  (invitation) varsågod
plunger vaskrensare
pocket n ficka
point of interest sevärdhet
police polis
police report polisrapport
police station polisstation
pond damm
post office postkontor
postage porto
postcard vykort
pot (cooking pot) gryta;
  (saucepan) kastrull
pound sterling engelsk pund
pregnant gravid
premium (gas) premium
prescription recept
price pris
print (computer) skriva ut
private privat
private room privatrum
problem problem
produce store matbutik
program (events) program
pub pub
public transportation allmänna
  kommunikationer
pull dra
purple lila
purpose syfte

purse (large) handväska, (small)
  portmonnä
push tryck
pushchair [BE] sittvagn

R

racket (tennis) racket
railroad järnväg
railway [BE] järnväg
rain regn
raincoat regnkappa
rap rap
rape n våldtäkt
rapids fors
rash n utslag
(disposable) razor (engångs)
  rakhyvel
reach v nå
read v läsa
ready färdig
receipt kvitto
receive v ta emot
receptionist receptionist
recommend v rekommendera
refrigderator kylskåp
region region
regular gas vanlig
relationship (romantic)
  förhållande
rent n hyra; v hyra
repair v reparera
repairs (car) reparationer
repeat v upprepa
report v (crime) anmäla
reservation bokning
reserved reserverad
rest area rastplats
restroom (sign) WC
restaurant restaurang
return v (give back) återlämna
return ticket [BE] retur (biljett)

reverse charge call [BE] ba-samtal
right (correct) rätt; **(direction)** höger
ring (jewelry) ring
river flod
road väg
road map vägkarta
romantic romantisk
room rum
room service rumservice
round n **(golf)** runda
round-trip ticket retur biljett
rubbish [BE] sopor

S

safe n kassaskåp
sailing segling
sandals sandaler
sanitary napkin binda
saucepan kastrull
sauna bastu
save v **(collect)** spara
scarf halsduk
schedule tidsschema
scissors sax
sea hav
seat (on train) plats
seat number platsnummer
seat reservation (train) sittplatsbiljett
seminar seminarium
send v skicka
separated (couple) separerad
service serveringsavgift
service charge (bank) expeditionsavgift
sex sex
shampoo shampoo
sheet lakan
shoe store skoaffär
shoes skor

shopping basket shoppingkorg
shopping cart shoppingvagn
shopping centre [BE] shoppingcenter
shopping mall shoppingcenter
shorts shorts
show v visa
shower dusch
sick sjuk
side effect biverkning
sightseeing tour sightseeingtur
sign v undertäckna
silk siden
SIM card (cell phone) SIM kort
single ticket [BE] enkel **(biljett)**
sit v sitta
size storlek
skiing skidåkning
skirt kjol
slice n skiva
slippers tofflor
slippery (icy) hal
slow adj långsam
small liten
sneakers träningsskor
snorkeling equipment snorkelutrustning
snow snö
snowboard snowboard
snowshoes pjäxor
soap tvål
soccer fotboll
sock socka
something något
soon snart
soother [BE] napp
sore throat halsont
sorry förlåt
south söder
souvenir souvenir
spa spa
spatula stekspade

speak *v* tala
spoon sked
sports massage
  träningsmassage
spouse (female) maka; (male)
  make
sprain stukning
square (town feature) torg
stadium stadion
stair trappa
stamp *n* frimärke
stamp your ticket stämpla er
  biljett
start *v* (car) starta
stay *n* stanna
steakhouse stekhus
steep brant
stolen stulen
stomach magen
stomachache ont i magen
stop *n* (bus stop) bushållplats;
  v stanna
store *n* butik; *v* förvara
strange konstig
stream å
street gata
stroller sittvagn
student studerande
study *v* läsa
stunning jättesnygg
subtitle text
suburb förort
subway tunnelbana
subway station
  tunnelbanestation
suitable lämplig
suitcase resväska
sunburn solbränna
sunglasses solglasögon
sunstroke solsting
super [BE] (gas) premium
supermarket snabbköp

surfboard surfbräda
sweater tröja
sweatshirt sweatshirt
Swedish *adj* svensk; (language)
  svenska
swelling svullnad
swim *v* simma
swimming pool simbassäng
swimming trunks badbyxor
swimsuit baddräkt
symbol (computer) tecken
symphony (orchestra) symfoni
synagogue synagoga

T

table bord
tablecloth duk
take *v* ta
take out *v* ta ut
taken (occupied) upptagen
tampon tampong
tax skatt
taxi taxi
teaspoon tesked
temperature temperatur
temple tempel
tennis tennis
tennis court tennisbana
terminal (airport) terminal
terrible förskräcklig
text message sms
textiles textil
thank you tack
theft rån
thief tjuv
think *v* tänka
ticket biljett
ticket machine biljettautomat
ticket office biljettkontor
tie *n* slips
tights [BE] strumpbyxor
timetable [BE] tidsschema

tip (service) dricks
tissue näsduk
to till
tobacconist tobaksaffär
toilet [BE] toalett; **(sign)** WC
toilet paper toalettpapper
tooth tand
toothbrush tandborste
toothpaste tandkräm
tour tur
tourist turist
tourist attraction turistattraktion
tourist information
   turistinformation
tourist office turistbyrå
town hall stadshus
toy store leksaksaffär
track (railroad) spår
trail spår
train *n* tåg
train station järnvägsstation
tram spårvagn
translate *v* översätta
travel *v* **(travel)** resa; **(drive)** åka
travel agency resebyrå
travel agent (female)
   resebyråkvinna; **(male)**
   resebyråman
travel sickness [BE] åksjuka
traveler's check resecheck
traveller's cheque [BE]
   resecheck
treat *v* **(to a meal)** bjuda
trim (hair) putsning
trip *n* resa
trolley [BE] bagagekärra
trouser [BE] byxor
try *v* prova
turn off *v* stänga av
turn on *v* sätta på

U

ugly ful
umbrella (standard) paraply;
   (sun) solparasol
underground [BE] tunnelbana
underground station [BE]
   tunnelbanestation
understand *v* förstå
underwear (general) underkläder
unfortunately tyvärr
United Kingdom Storbritanien
unlimited (mileage) obegränsad
until tills
urgent brådskande
United State Förenta Staterna
use *v* använda
username användarnamn
utensil bestick

V

vacancy ledigt rum
vacation semester
vacuum cleaner dammsugare
vaginal infection vaginal
   infektion
valley dal
valuable värdesak
value *n* värde
vegetarian vegetarian
viewpoint utsiktspunkt
village by
visit *n* besök; *v* besöka
visiting hours besökstid
visitor besökare
visitor besökare
visually impaired syn skadad
vomit *v* kräkas

W

wait vänta
wake up *v* vakna

wake-up call telefonväckning
walk n promenad; v gå
wallet plånbok
want v vilja
washing machine tvättmaskin
waterfall vattenfall
weather forecast
   väderleksrapport
weekend helg
welcome välkommen
west väster
wheelchair rullstol
wheelchair ramp rullstolsramp
when när
where var
which vilken
white vitt
who vem
widow änka
widower änkling
window fönster

window seat fönsterplats
windsurfing vindsurfa
wireless internet trådlös internet
with med
withdrawal (bank) uttag
wood trä
wool ull
work from home v arbeta
   hemifrån
wrap v (present) slå in
write v skriva
wrong fel

Y

yellow gul
yes ja
yield lämna företräde
youth hostel vandrarhem

Z

zoo djurpark

SWEDISH–ENGLISH

A

acceptera v accept
adapter adapter
adoptera v adopt
adress n address
advokat lawyer
affärscentrum shopping mall
   [centre BE]
affärsresa business trip
akupunktur acupuncture
alla all
allergi allergy
allergisk allergic
allergisk reaktion allergic
   reaction

allmänna
kommunikationer public
   transportation
alternativ väg alternate route
aluminiumfolie aluminum foil
ambulans ambulance
amma v breastfeed
andas breathe
andra other
anemisk anemic
anfall n attack
anknytning extension (phone)
ankomst arrival
anlända v arrive
anmäla v report (crime)

annan another
antikaffär antiques store
antiseptisk salva antiseptic cream
använda v use
användarnamn username
apotek pharmacy [chemist BE]
apparat appliance
arbeta hemifrån v work from home
armband bracelet
aroma-terapi aromatherapy
astma asthma
audioguide audio guide
automatisk automatic
av off
avancerad expert
avbeställa v cancel
avgå v depart (plane)
avgång departure
avgångsgate departure gate

B

baby baby
bad bath
badbyxor swim trunks
baddräkt swim suit
badrum bathroom [toilet BE]
bagagekärra baggage cart [trolley BE]
bagageutlämning baggage claim
bageri bakery
bakom behind
band band (music group)
bank bank
bankavgift bank charge
bankkort debit card
Bankomat ATM
bar bar
bara only (just)
barn child

barnbassäng kiddie pool [paddling pool BE]
barnmeny children's menu
barnstol highchair
barnsäng crib [child's cot BE]
barnvakt babysitter
bastu sauna
batteri battery
be om ursäkt v apologize
behå bra
behålla v keep
behöva v need
bekräfta v confirm (reservation)
bensin gasoline [petrol BE]
bensinstation gas station [petrol station BE]
berg mountain
bergklättring rock climbing
bestick utensil
beställa v order
besök n visit
besöka v visit
besökare visitor
besökstid visiting hours
betala v pay
bett n bite
betyda mean (signify)
bibliotek library
bikini bikini
bil car
bilbarnstol car seat
bildäck car deck (ferry)
bilfärja car ferry
biljett ticket
biljettautomat ticket machine
biljettkontor ticket office
biljettpris fare
billig cheap
bilsäte car seat
biluthyrning car rental
binda sanitary napkin [towel BE]
bio movies [cinema BE]

bit piece
bita v bite
biverkning side effect
bjuda v treat (to a meal)
blankett n form
bli v become
blod blood
blodtryck blood pressure
blus blouse
blöda bleed
blöja diaper [nappy BE]
bo v live
boardingkort boarding pass
bok book
bokhandel bookstore
bokning reservation (travel, restaurant)
bomull cotton
bondgård farm
bord table
borda v board (flight)
botanisk trädgård botanical garden
bra adj good
brandutgång fire exit
brant steep
bredvid next to
brev letter
brinna v burn
bro bridge
brosch brooch
brun brown
brådskande urgent
bröstet chest
burk n can
businesscenter business center
buss bus
busshållplats bus stop [request stop BE]
busslinje bus route
bussterminal bus station
butik n store

by village
byta v change (baby, connection)
byxor pants [trouser BE]
båt boat
båttur boat tour
börja v begin

C

centrum downtown
checka in check in (airport)
checka ut check out (hotel)
chef manager
cigarr cigar
cykel bicycle
cykelåkning cycling
cykelås bicycle lock

D

dagsbiljett day ticket
dagstur day trip
dal valley
dalahäst dala horse
damfrisör hairdresser
damkläder ladieswear
damtoalett ladies' restroom
damm pond
dammsugare vacuum cleaner
dansa v dance
dator computer
dela divide
delikatessaffär delicatessen
denim denim
deodorant deodorant
diabetiker n diabetic
diamant diamond
diarré diarrhea
diesel diesel
digital digital
digitalt kort digital print
diskmedel dish detergent
diskmaskin dishwasher
djup deep

djup tallrik bowl
djur animal
djurpark zoo
docka doll
doktor doctor
dollar dollar
dosering dosage
dra pull
dricks tip (service)
droppar drops (medication)
dubbad dubbed
duk table cloth
dusch shower
dyka v dive
dykarutrustning diving
  equipment
dyr expensive
dålig bad
dörr door
döv deaf

E

e-biljett e-ticket
efter after
ej no (do not...)
eller or
endast only (nothing but)
engelska English
engelsk pund pound sterling
engångskamera disposable
  camera
enkel biljett one-way trip [single
  ticket BE]
enkelriktad one way (street)
enter enter (computer)
e-post e-mail
e-postadress e-mail address
europeiska unionen European
  Union (EU)
expeditionsavgift service charge
  (bank)
express express

expresspost express mail
expressutdelning overnight
  delivery (mail)

F

familj family
fantastisk adj fantastic
fast pris fixed price
fax fax
fax machine fax machine
feber fever
fel wrong
ficka n pocket
film movie [film BE]
fiske fishing
flaska bottle
flasköppnare bottle opener
flerdagskort multi-day card
flickvän girlfriend
flod river
flyg flight
flygbolag airline
flygnummer flightnumber
flygplats airport
flygpost airmail
fläkt fan
fm a.m.
fontän fountain
fors rapids
fort fast
fotboll soccer [football BE]
fotgängare pedestrian
foto photo
framkalla v develop (photos)
fri free
frimärken stamps
frisyr hair style
fru Mrs.
frys freezer
fråga ask
från from...
fröken Miss

ful ugly
fungera v function (work)
fylla v fill
fält field
färdig ready
färg color
färja ferry
födelsedag birthday
fönster window
fönsterplats window seat
för tung/stor too much, excess (baggage)
före before
Förenta Staterna United States
föreställning performance (music, theater)
förhållande relationship (romantic)
förlora v lose
förlåt sorry
försening n delay
förskräcklig terrible
förskylning cold (sick)
första first
förstå v understand
försäkring insurance
förtulla v declare (customs)
förvaringsskåp luggage locker
förort suburb

G

gaffel fork
gammal adj old, n age
gasbinda bandage (gauze)
gata street
gate gate (boarding)
ge v give
gift married
gilla v like
glas glass (drinking)
glasögon eyeglasses
glödlampa light bulb

glömma v forget
godkänna v approve
golf golf
golfbana golf course
golfklubb golf club
gratis free of charge
gravera v engrave
gravid pregnant
grotta cave
grupp group
gryta pot (cooking)
guide guide (brochure); guide (person)
gul yellow
guld gold
gullig adj cute
gym gym
gå v walk, leave
gå sönder break; breakdown (car)
gärna adj desire
göra v do

H

ha v have
hal slippery (icy)
halsband necklace
halsduk scarf
halsont sore throat
halv halv
handbagage carry on
handgjord handmade
handicappanpassad toalett handicapped accessible toilet [disabled BE]
handpenning deposit
handväska purse [hand bag BE]
hantverk handicraft
hatt hat
hav sea
hej hi
hej då goodbye
helg weekend

helgdag holiday (celebration)
hemifrån work from home
hemlagad homemade (food)
herr Mr.
herrfrisör barber
herrkläder menswear
herrtoalett men's restroom
iss elevator [lift BE]
hittegodsexpedition lost-and-found [lost property office BE]
hjälm helmet
hjälp n help
hjälpa v help
hosta n cough; v to cough
hotell hotel
huvudvärkstablett aspirin
hyra rent [hire BE]
hårbalsam conditioner
hårborste hairbrush
hårspray hairspray
hårtork hair dryer
hälsokostaffär health food store
hämta v pick up (thing/person)
händelse event
här here
höger right (direction)
hörselskadad hearing impaired

I

i in
ibuprofen ibuprofen
ID-kort identification
ifrån from
incheckning check in desk (airport)
information information desk
ingen nobody (sg)
inget nothing
ingång entrance
inkluderad included (in the price)
innehålla contain

inomhusbassäng indoor swimming pool
inrikes domestic (travel)
inrikes flyg domestic flight
insekt insect
insektbett insect bite
instant messenger instant messenger
instruktör instructor
inte not
inte inkluderad not included (in the price)
internationellt körkort international driver's license
internet internet
internetkafé internet café
intressant interesting
inuti inside
ishockey ice hockey
iväg away

J

ja yes
jacka jacket
jeans jeans
jetski jet ski
jobb job
juvelerare jeweler
järnväg railroad [railway BE]
järnvägsstation train station
jättesnygg stunning

K

kafé café
kalender calendar
kall cold (temperature)
kam comb
kamera camera
kan v can (be able to)
karaff carafe
karta map

kasino casino
kassaskåp n safe
kassör cashier (male)
kassörska cashier (female)
kastrull saucepan (cooking)
katedral cathedral
kemisk toalett chemical toilet
kemtvätt dry cleaner
keramik ceramics
kjol skirt
klassiskmusik classical music
klippa cliff
klippning hair cut
klocka(n) clock
klädaffär clothing store
klädsel dress code
klänning dress
kniv knife
kokmöjligheter cooking facilities
kollega colleague
komma v come
konditori coffee shop
kondom condom
konferens conference
konferensrum conference room
kongresshall convention hall
konsert concert
konservöppnare can opener
konstig strange
kontaktlinsvätska contact lens
   solution
kontant n cash
kopia n copy
kopieringsautomat copy
   machine
kopp cup
korkskruv corkscrew
kort n card, adj short
kosta v cost
kostym suit (jacket/pants)
kreditkort credit card
kristallglas crystal (glass)

krona krona (Swedish currency)
kräkas v vomit
kudde pillow
kulle hill
kulspetspenna pen
kultur culture
kuvertavgift cover charge
kvinna female
kvitto receipt
kylskåp refrigerator
kyrka church
kyssa v kiss
kök kitchen
köpa v buy
köra drive
körkort driver's license

L

laga v fix
lakan sheet
laktosintolerant lactose
   intolerant
lampa light (lamp)
landsnummer country code
ledarhund guide dog
ledig available
ledigt rum vacancy
legitimation identification
lekplats playground
lekrum playpen
leksaksaffär toy store
lektion lesson
liftkort liftpass
lila purple
linje line
linne linen
liten small
livbåt life boat
livräddare lifeguard
livsmedelsaffär grocery store
   [greengrocer BE]
loafers loafers

logga in log on (connect to internet)
logga ut log out
logi accommodation
lotto lottery
luftkonditionering air conditioning
lugn calm
lust n desire
lyft lift (ski)
lång long
långsam slow
låsa v lock
läder leather
lägenhet apartment [flat BE]
lämna v leave
lämna före träde yield
lämplig suitable
längdåkning cross country skiing
länge long (time)
läsa v (book) read; (school) study
lätt easy
lösenord password

M

magen stomach
maka spouse (female)
make spouse (male)
man husband, man
manikyr manicure
marknad market
matbutik produce store (general store) [grocer BE]
med with
meddelande message
medicin medicine
medium medium
mellan between
men but
mens menstruation
mensvärk menstrual cramps
meny menu

mikrovågsugn microwave
minimum minimum (requirement)
minneskort memory card
misstag mistake
mitt emot opposite
mobiltelefon cell phone [mobile phone BE]
moms sales tax [VAT BE]
moped moped
moské mosque
motel motel
motorcykel motorcycle
motorbåt motorboat
motorväg highway [motorway BE]
mun mouth
museum museum
mygg olja insect repellent
mynt coin
måltid meal
många many
måste must
måttsked measuring spoon
mässan mass (catholic)

N

nagelfil nail file
nagelvårdssalong nail salon
namn n name
napp pacifier [soother BE]
nappflaska baby bottle
naturreservat nature reserve
norr north
nota bill (restaurant)
nummer number
ny new
nyckel key
nyckelkort key card
nå v reach
någon anyone
något anything, something
när when
nära nearby

näsduk tissue
nästa next
nätuttag electrical outlet
nödbroms emergency brake
nödsituation emergency
nödutgång emergency exit
nöjesfält amusement park

O

obegränsad unlimited (mileage)
och and
olycka accident
omkring about (approximately)
ont i magen stomachache
opera opera
optiker optician
orkester orchestra

P

paket package [parcel BE]
panorama panorama
papperservett paper napkin
paracetamol acetaminophen
paraply umbrella
park park
parkering parking
parkering på gatan street
   parking
parkeringsplats (one or several)
   parking lot [car park BE]
pass passport
passa v fit
passkontroll passport control
pedikyr pedicure
pensionat boarding house
per per
per dag per day
per vecka per week
person person
petit petite
picknickområde picnic area
PIN kod PIN code

pjäxor snowshoes
plan n plan
plastfolie plastic wrap [cling film
   BE]
platina platinum
plats seat (on train)
plats i mittgången aisle seat
platsnummer seat number
plattform platform (train)
plomb filling
plånbok wallet
pojke boy
pojkvän boyfriend
polis police
polisrapport police report
polisstation police station
porto postage
post mail
postkontor post office
postlåda mail box
premium premium [super BE]
   (gas)
presentaffär gift shop
present gift
preventivmedel contraceptive
pris price
privat private
privatrum private room
problem problem
program progam (events)
prova v try
provrum fitting room
pub pub
putsning trim (hair)
pyjamas pajamas
på on (switch)
påse bag
pärla pearl

R

rabatt discount
rabattkort discount card

racket racket (tennis)
radera delete (computer)
(engångs)rakhyvel (disposable) razor
rap rap
rastplats rest area
recept prescription
receptionist receptionist
region region
regn rain
regnkappa raincoat
rekommendera v recommend
ren adj clean
rensa clear (computer, ATM), clean
reparationer repairs (car)
reparera v repair
resa v travel, n trip
resebyrå travel agency
resebyråkvinna travel agent (female)
resebyråman travel agent (male)
resecheck traveler's check [traveller's cheque BE]
reserverad reserved
restaurang restaurant
resväska suitcase
retur (biljett) round-trip ticket [return ticket BE]
ridsport horseback riding
riktnummer area code
ring ring (jewelry)
ringa v call (phone)
rock coat
rolig fun
romantisk romantic
rosa pink
rullstol wheelchair
rullstolsramp wheelchair ramp
rulltrappa escalator
rum room
rumservice room service

runda v round (golf)
ryggsäck backpack
rån theft
räkning bill (hotel, invoice)
rätt correct
rökning förbjuden no smoking
rörelsehindrad disabled

S

sambo domestic partner
sammanträde meeting
samtal phone call
sandaler sandals
sax scissors
sedel banknote
segling sailing
semester vacation
seminarium seminar
sen late
separerad separated (couple)
serveringsavgift service
servett napkin
sevärdhet point of interest
sex sex
shampoo shampoo
shoppingcenter shopping mall [shopping centre BE]
shoppingkorg shopping basket
shoppingvagn shopping cart
shorts shorts
siden silk
sightseeingtur sightseeing tour
simbassäng swimming pool
SIM kort SIM card (cell phone)
simma v swim
sista last
sitta v sit
sittplatsbiljett seat reservation (train)
sittvagn stroller [pushchair BE]
sjuk sick [ill BE]
sjukhus hospital

sjuksköterska nurse
sjö lake
skada n damage, v harm
skatt tax
sked spoon
skicka v send
skidåkning skiing
skild divorced
skiva n slice
skoaffär shoe store
skog forest
skor shoes
skriva write
skriva ut print
skurmop n mop
skyldig innocent
skärp belt
slagfält battlefield
slips tie
slott castle
slå v (phone number) dial
slå in v wrap (present)
sms text message
smutsig dirty
smycken jewelry
snabbköp supermarket
snabbtvätt Laundromat [launderette BE]
snart soon
snorkelutrustning snorkeling equipment
snowboard snowboard
snäll adj nice
snälla (request) please
snö snow
socka sock
solbränna sunburn
solglasögon sunglasses
solsting sunstroke
solstol deck chair
sopborste broom

sopor garbage (garbage disposal) [rubbish BE]
soppåse garbage bag
souvenir souvenir
spa spa
spara v save
specifierad räkning itemized bill
spel game
spela v play
spets lace
spår trail [piste BE]; track (railroad)
spårvagn tram
stad city
stadion stadium
stadshus town hall
stadskarta city map
stanna n stay; v stop
starta v start
stekhus steakhouse
stekpanna frying pan
stekspade spatula
stiga av get off (train)
stollift chair lift
stor big
Storbritannien United Kingdom
storlek size
strand beach
strumpbyxor panty hose [tights BE]
strykjärn iron (clothes)
studerande student
stuga cabin
stukning n sprain
stulen stolen
städutrustning cleaning supplies
ställe place
stämpla er biljett stamp your ticket
stäng av turn off
stänga v close
stängt closed
störa disturb

stövlar boots
summa amount
surfbräda surfboard
sval cool (temperature)
svart black
sweatshirt sweatshirt
svensk *adj* swedish
svenska *adj* swedish; (language) Swedish
svullnad swelling
svårt difficult
syfte purpose
symfoni symphony (orchestra)
syn skadad visually impaired
synagoga synagogue
syrebehandling oxygen treatment
syssla med *v* do (work with)
sällskap company (companionship)
säng bed
sätta på turn on
söder south
sönder broken

T

ta *v* take
ta emot *v* receive
ta med bring
ta ut take out
tablett pill (tablet)
tack thank you
tala *v* speak
tallrik plate
tampong tampon
tand tooth
tandborste toothbrush
tandkräm toothpaste
tandläkare dentist
tandprotes dentures
tappa *v* lose; drop
taxfri duty free
taxfri vara duty free good

taxi taxi
teaterpjäs play (theater)
tecken symbol (computer)
telefon katalog telephone catalog
telefonautomat pay phone
telefonkort phone card
telefonnummer phone number
telefonväckning wake up call
temperatur temperature
tempel temple
tenn pewter
tennis tennis
tennisbana tennis court
terminal terminal (airport)
tesked teaspoon
text subtitle
textil textiles
tidning newspaper
tidningskiosk newsstand
tidsschema schedule [timetable BE]
till to
tills until
tillåta *v* allow
timme hour
toalett bathroom [toilet BE]
toalettpapper toilet paper
tobaksaffär tobacconist
tofflor slippers
tolk interpreter
top peak (moutain)
torg square (town feature)
trappa stair
trasig broken (damaged)
trevlig pleasant
trist boring
tryck push
trådlös internet wireless internet
trä wood
träffa *v* meet
träfigur wood carvings

iv wooden knife
...ingsmassage sports massage
träningsskor sneakers
träsked wooden spoon
träskor wooden clogs
tröja sweater
tugga v chew
tull customs
tulldeklaration customs declaration form
tunnelbana subway [underground BE]
tunnelbanestation subway station [underground station BE]
tur tour
turist tourist
turist klass economy class
turistattraktion tourist attraction
turistbyrå tourist office
turistinformation tourist information
tvål soap
tvätt laundry
tvättmaskin washing machine
tvättmedel laundry detergent
tvättmöjligheter laundry facilities
tyg fabric
tyvärr unfortunately
tåg train
täcke n blanket
tältsäng camping bed
tändare lighter
tändsticka match (fire)
tänka v think

U

ull wool
underhållning entertainment
underkläder underwear (general)
undersöka v examine (medical)
undertäckna v sign

upprepa v repeat
upptagen busy
ursäkta v excuse me (to get attention, pardon me)
ursäkta mig excuse me (to get past)
ute outside
utgång exit way out
utländsk valuta foreign currency
utomhus outdoor
utomhusbassäng outdoor pool
utrikes international (travel)
utrustning equipment
utsiktspunkt view point
utslag n rash
uttag withdrawal (bank)

V

vacker beautiful
vaginal infektion vaginal infection
vakna v wake up
valuta currency
vandra v hike
vandrarhem youth hostel
vandring hiking
vanlig regular gas
var where
var god stör ej do not disturb
vara v be
varje each
varm hot
varsågod (invitation) please
varuhus department store
vaskrensare plunger
vattenfall waterfall
WC (sign) restroom [toilet BE]
veckotidning magazine
vegetarian vegetarian
vem who
vid at
vilja v want

vilken which
vilse lost
visa v show
vitrin display case
vitt white
vykort postcard
våldtäkt n rape
våning floor (level, etage in building)
våtservetter för barn baby wipes
väderleksrapport weather forecast
väg road
vägkarta road map
välkommen welcome
välling baby formula
vän friend
vänster left (direction)
vänta wait
värde n value
värdesak n valuable
värme heat
väska bag
väster west
växel n change (money)
växelkontor currency exchange office
växelkursen exchange rate
växla change money

Y

yr dizzy
ytterligare further (more)

Å

å stream
åka v travel, drive (motor vehicle)
åksjuka motion sickness [travel sickness BE]
ålder age
återlämna v return (give back)
äkta authentic

äkthetsbevis certificate of authenticity
älska v love
ändra v change (reservation)
ändra på v alter
änka widow
änkling widower
äta v eat

Ö

ögonblick (one) moment
öppet open
öppettider business hours [opening hours BE]
öppna v open
öra ear
öre öre (Swedish currency)
örhänge earring
öster east
över across (the road)
överfall mugging
övergångsställe för fotgängare pedestrian crossing
översätta v translate
övervikstbagage excess baggage